The Front Line Guide to CREATING A WINNING MANAGEMENT STYLE

Woodrow H. Sears

HRD Press, Inc. • Amherst • Massachusetts

Copyright © 2007, HRD Press, Inc.

Published by:

HRD Press, Inc.
22 Amherst Road
Amherst, MA 01002
800-822-2801 (U.S. and Canada)
413-253-3488
413-253-3490 (fax)
www.hrdpress.com

ISBN 0-87425-937-1

Production services by Jean Miller
Editorial services by Suzanne Bay
Cover design by Eileen Klockars

DEDICATION

For Andrew Graves, MSgt. U.S.A.F. (Ret.):
A master manager who energizes and *involves*
wherever he works.

Table of Contents

Preface ix

Introduction xi

Chapter 1: A Short History of the Search
for Higher Productivity 1
   Management Style is "Discovered" 2
   A Matter of Beliefs 3

Chapter 2: Managers Make the Difference 5

Chapter 3: Identifying Payoff Behaviors 7

Chapter 4: Overcoming Worker Resistance 13
   Reinterpreting McGregor 16
   Another View of Theory X 18

Chapter 5: Developing Competence through
Performance-Specific Feedback 23
   Communication Skills: Prerequisites for a Winning
      Management Style 24
   Relationships Are Built on Shared Information 26
   Welcome to the World of Responsible Adults 27
   What about Power and Authority? 29
   About Developing Competence 30
   A View of Management Styles 34
   Giving Situation-Specific Feedback 36

Chapter 6: Building Respect for Self, Team, and Company 39

In Times of Change… 40

Building Self-Respect and Self-Esteem 42

Building Respect within the Team 45

Building Respect for the Company 49

Chapter 7: Redefining Roles and Responsibilities 53

All Tasks Must be Performed Satisfactorily 54

That Includes the Manager's Role, Too 56

Chapter 8: Rewarding and Promoting 59

The Mysterious "They" and "Them" 60

Finding Advancement in a Flat Organization 61

The Manager as Mentor 63

Chapter 9: As the Running Shoe People Say… 67

Just do it! 69

People with Winning Management Styles 70

Chapter 10: Your Communication Style 73

Empathy and Communication Style:
Being Accessible to Others 76

Critical Ability and Communication Style 79

Searching and Communication Style 81

Advising Others 84

Mentoring 85

Summing It All Up 86

Chapter 11: Your Personal Style 89

Feelings and Personal Style 89

Thinking and Personal Style 92

Sensing and Personal Style 95

Intuition and Personal Style 97

One More Element of Personal Style 97

Chapter 12: Coming to Grips with Management Style 101

    A Crazy Idea 103

    It's as Simple as You Want to Make It 104

    Other Paths to Theory Y 105

Chapter 13: Wrapping Up 109

    Finding a Safe Place to Try on New Behaviors 109

    A Few Words about Ethics 111

    Now, Go Do It! 112

References 113

About the Author 115

Preface

This book was developed to achieve two purposes: First, I wanted to present the concept of "management style" as an identifiable, observable, and replicable set of attributes that are reflected in the behavior of managers as they deal with tasks and employees. An individual's management style reflects his or her personal beliefs and values; it is a blend of prescribed social behaviors that have been filtered or modified by what we know in our gut is the right thing to do. Regardless of the component values and behaviors of your management style, we can all make incremental improvements that will help us be more effective with those we work with and, of no less importance, with our families.

My second purpose for writing this book is to relate this discussion of important managerial behaviors to research-based developmental programs such as the Managerial Assessment of Proficiency. Research involving thousands of managers in some of America's leading professional, commercial, industrial, and military organizations identified specific behaviors that can and do lead to managerial excellence—behaviors that can be acquired by anyone reading this book. Developers of such managerial development programs validate their findings in a cross-section of corporate settings. The component competencies and values presented here have since become the *de facto* standard or starting point when an organization seeks to improve managerial performance.

The information in this book is not meant as a substitute for participation in a solid managerial assessment program, but it will reassure readers that creating a winning management style is well within their capabilities. This book will show you how to do it.

Introduction

One of the things we know about human behavior is that it is generally predictable. When you itch, you scratch—and the people who know you and watch your behavior can predict *how* you will scratch your itches. They know more about your behavior than you think.

Few people watch anyone as closely as workers watch their managers. They look for the cues and clues that allow them to figure out the manager's mood. This is worker self-defense: Workers try to learn the best ways to approach their manager, and how and when to avoid him or her until certain moods pass. It's survival.

A winning management style is not about becoming *less* predictable, but about becoming more consistent and more congruent and removing the barriers between you and the people you manage. People won't have to waste their energy trying to read your moods, so they'll know what to do and how to respond.

For better or worse, you already have a management style or a set of patterned behaviors that you use in dealing with people and situations. This book will provide the tools you'll need to change your patterns so you can create a winning management style and become a more-effective manager.

I want to help you to create more value, more products, and more profit in your role as a manager. Yes, it is probable that you will be more popular with co-workers and enjoy your job more if you use what you learn in this Guide, but that is a happy by-product. Optimizing your effectiveness is the goal!

Woody Sears
Vilnius, Lithuania

Chapter 1

A Short History of the Search for Higher Productivity

The cost of labor is a major expense in most organizations (if not the largest). The question on every leader's mind is how to improve the return on investment of all that money spent on people.

Scientific management—that is, how to get more productivity and return on investment (ROI) from workers—didn't exist until about 100 years ago, when Frederick W. Taylor used his powers of observation to figure out a way to increase worker productivity. Taylor redesigned the shovel being used by mine workers. Using a large, energetic Polish worker as his model, Taylor measured the amount of coal shoveled in a day using the traditional shovel. Then, the worker spent a day with Taylor's shovel and moved 40 percent more coal. Scientific management was born! Taylor is now widely considered to be the father of Scientific Management and Systems Engineering as a discipline.

Taylor's research was followed by decades of time studies in which workers were treated more like machines than humans. Naturally, this provided fertile ground for union organization and virtually institutionalized hard dividing lines between labor and management. Regulations to prevent worker abuse evolved into absurd rules that often limited productivity, further hardening the lines of antagonism between the two sides.

But around 1932, something unexpected happened at the Western Electric plant in Hawthorne, Illinois. In a series of experiments conducted under the direction of Elton Mayo of Harvard University, researchers discovered that one group of women in the study consistently produced more than their managers expected of them, regardless of working conditions. Why?

The surprising answer was that *the women felt special.* Someone was paying attention to them![1]

The so-called Scientific Management movement began to give way to the Human Potential movement, which held that if people work more when someone pays attention to them, then *every* work group needs someone to pay attention to them. Obviously, it is the manager/supervisor/foreman who should be making workers feel good, but it is tough to overcome generations of cultural norms. Years of labor-management conflict created those hard lines between workers and managers: Workers expected to be mistreated, and managers believed that workers would not produce unless they were punished and treated harshly. Weak managers didn't last long.

Management Style is "Discovered"

This standoff continued for almost 30 years, until Douglas McGregor published his book *The Human Side of Enterprise* in 1960. McGregor provided a conceptual lens that illuminated the subject of hard and soft management, and nothing has been done since that makes the differences clearer or puts the focus more directly on management and management style.

Simply put, McGregor's studies revealed that managers could be divided into two groups: Theory X managers, and Theory Y managers. Theory X managers, he said, believe that workers are lazy, avoid responsibility, and won't produce unless threatened and treated harshly. Under Theory X, the productive force is rooted in management, not in the workers.

The other group described by McGregor was composed of what he called Theory Y managers: men and women who believe that people are capable of self-discipline and high levels of productivity if they receive management support. But there is more to Theory Y than this, and management *style* is an important element.

McGregor found that Theory Y managers tend to be more demanding, require people to work up to their capacities, and provide support to ensure that they perform. This casts the manager in a non-traditional, facilitating, cheerleading role in which they are responsible for giving workers what they need to perform and then getting out of their way.

A Matter of Beliefs

McGregor's work took management into a new realm that went beyond the traditional functions of plan, organize, direct, supervise, control, report, and budget first outlined by Henri Fayol in the 1920s.[2] Indeed, management took on an almost mystical guise as soon as people began looking at McGregor's contention that it is their beliefs about people that make Theory Y managers function differently.

McGregor's position was that belief in people—in their decency, their honesty, and their desire to contribute—is essential in management. Without such faith, it would not be possible for a manager to use his or her motivating skills to get individuals to perform at levels consistent with their abilities. McGregor's research convinced him that people can become excited about and committed to the work they do. More recent studies among minimum-wage custodial crews demonstrate anew the fact that regardless of income level, people are capable of group loyalty and meritorious levels of performance. All they need is someone to believe in them and to tell them that they're important.

Chapter 1 Notes

1. The Hawthorne Studies were conducted between 1927-1932 under the direction of Elton Mayo of Harvard. The unexpected results changed the course of management research.

2. Henri Fayol's work was not published in English until 1949.

Chapter 2

Managers Make the Difference

McGregor and other researchers made the point that managers can make a positive difference by releasing the energies of workers that are being withheld during the workday. The premise of this book is that most managers miss the opportunity to make the kinds of positive differences they have the potential to make because they lack the basic beliefs or skills or imagination that are critical if you want to effectively energize groups of individuals.

This creates major opportunities for readers, because every suggestion here is do-able. Access to the information you need to create a winning management style and to become an exceptional manager is in your hands. The path to career advancement is spelled out in the pages that follow.

Creating a winning management style is the result of packaging the interpersonal attributes that make managers effective. Begin by thinking about times when you were really happy at work. What was going on? Most likely, it was when you and your co-workers were overcoming obstacles to meet a tight deadline, your manager was there working with you, and everyone shared cake and coffee or pizza to celebrate a victory over impossible odds.

Have there been times like that? If so, what factors did they have in common? Perhaps these things:

- People felt good about themselves.
- Everyone worked together with enthusiasm.

- People helped each other with good humor.
- Everyone really pushed to meet the deadline.

When the pressure was off, everyone kicked back and relaxed, laughing and hugging one another to celebrate a job well done.

And one more thing: The manager did not get in the way, and *that* is a very big point! Often, workers know so much more than their managers about the jobs they do, the equipment they operate, and the office routines they have to follow that it's positively insulting for a manager to give them directions.

If you have had these kinds of experiences and you want to create the same working conditions for others, you have taken the first big step toward creating a winning management style.

Chapter 3

Identifying Payoff Behaviors

Have you ever worked for someone you would consider to be the "perfect" boss? Those who have say that going to work becomes a pleasure—something to look forward to, rather than something to dread. In our effort to describe a winning management style, we've looked at mindset and management philosophy. In this chapter, we turn to how managers treat their employees, and how these interactions affect productivity.

What is your idea of the "perfect" boss? Maybe he or she demonstrates these behaviors:

He treats me with respect.

She does not speak as though I don't know my job.

He asks for my opinion about work issues.

She says "Please" and "Thank you."

He expresses appreciation for work done well and on time.

She lets me know about training courses that might be good for me.

He is willing to admit his mistakes.

She never rebukes people for errors.

He focuses on solutions, instead of looking for someone to blame.

She notices when people are stressed or are having work or personal problems.

He is sensitive and supportive when people have family problems.

She compliments people on new hair styles, new clothes, etc.

He coaches people who are having trouble with a task.

When overtime is necessary, he or she is there, too.

He is willing to acknowledge and identify outstanding performance.

She is willing to support capable individuals when promotions are possible.

He is open to suggestions regarding changes or improvements in office or plant processes.

She works as hard as we do.

He demonstrates pleasure in working with us.

She infuses the work group with the confidence to excel.

He helps people decide whether or not to leave the organization if they cannot meet performance standards.

If a manager does all these things consistently, it's fair to say that he or she uses a truly admirable management style—one that frees co-workers for extraordinary productivity.

If you are committed to becoming an exemplary manager, you no doubt want to do every one of these things. However, you'll first have to overcome one obstacle: lack of trust. Workers tend to be reluctant to trust a new manager. Almost every worker has felt misused or abused at some point, so it's no surprise that they are somewhat cautious with a new manager or a manager who wants to work with them in a different way. This is *the dark side* of organizational culture at work!

There are few places where people are more distrustful than in the former Soviet Union, a collection of societies in which people learn to trust no one outside their immediate family or their extended family (a *de facto* clan). If someone is not a member of either of these groups, you don't take them into your home. I was fortunate enough to be invited to one clan's day-after-Christmas dinner, a gathering of more than 20 middle-aged siblings, in-laws, cousins, and friends from university days. A friend explained what tied these individuals together: "These are the people we can depend on during the dark times. You might not like them all equally, but we trust each other, and have proved that we can."

When my friend Andy Graves first arrived in Vladivostok to work for the U.S. Consulate, he discovered that none of the locally employed staff (Russians) had ever been in the home of an American co-worker. So several months later, he organized a party in his home at Thanksgiving, complete with music by a local combo, and invited his entire staff and their spouses. Staff members were surprised and suspicious, and only a few showed up. He demanded to know where the rest of them were, and was told that they were afraid to come. Then, reverting to language and a management style more characteristic of his previous role as a U.S.A.F. master sergeant, he ordered his guests to track down the missing staff and to "...get them here. You tell them that as far as I'm concerned, this is a work day, and they're going to have a really unhappy boss if I don't see them here—and with their spouses. Pronto!"

Of course, dinner was delayed, but with turkey, it hardly matters—you just heat up the gravy. Everyone showed up. The combo played jazz, there were many toasts, a lot of vodka was knocked back (along with about a case of American wine), and Andy's staff learned a wonderful lesson: *They were important enough to be guests in his home.* The fact that such an invitation would never be extended by any Russian boss they knew of was not lost on the guests. That evening marked the beginning of new working relationships for most of them.

There are going to be a few people in any organization who are fearful or resistant to change. You can't make people trust you, but you can create opportunities for them to see you in settings in which trust is implicit. I made an effort to provide a similar lesson when I was teaching in an MBA program for the banking community in San Francisco. An MBA degree was considered a ticket to advancement, so unless another student was a co-worker, everyone viewed everyone else as a competitor, rather than as a resource person with a common objective. That restricted the kind of cooperation my teaching style requires, so I fought back with the best weapon at my disposal: I made them socialize and get to know each other. On the first night of class, I gave them an option for the final exam: They could have a written final, with exam questions posted two weeks in advance, or they could have a party. But if they chose a party, (1) they all had to organize it, and (2) everyone had to come with their spouse or a significant other—and only a death in the family would be an acceptable excuse for missing the "exam." We had some wonderful parties, including a picnic in Golden Gate Park, and many of the spouses expressed appreciation for their first invitation to be involved in the academic program that was taking so much time and family money. Several times during the semester, I would liven-up breaks during those evening courses by having someone bring in coffee and boxes of doughnuts, at my own expense (which was something really non-traditional!).

Every manager wants more and better performance from staff members, but the important question is this:

> What are you willing to give in order to get
> more from your employees?

Just like you did when you were a kid, if you make the dare, you have to go first.

Management style is a reflection of one's own values, translated into action and involvement (or lack of) with your staff. You can only be as authentic/vulnerable/involved as your own values will permit, and you can be attentive to others only to the degree that your own self-absorption permits. Then you can't fool people with nice words and occasional gestures. They know who you are and what you believe, and what they think about you is more accurate than you can imagine.

Chapter 4

Overcoming Worker Resistance

A manager with a winning management style cannot work his or her magic until workers are convinced that the manager is credible. But convincing distrustful workers is a difficult challenge; too often, employees reinforce existing barriers to cooperation by reminding themselves of how things *really* work, which managers to avoid, and which mistakes not to make, as well as by retelling various tales of misfortunes about people recently fired and certain hard truths about relations with management (folklore).

Every lie ever told by a manager, every trusting employee who was sandbagged by a dishonest manager, and every employee suggestion that was co-opted by the employee's own manager are all part of the folklore package.

Folklore is the life-blood of culture, the collection of anecdotal evidence that describes "how things really work around here." It includes stories of almost-mythic proportions about victims of the system (*"Remember what happened to Fred Smith!"*). Such remembrances are as full of meaning for insiders as the World War II motto, "Remember Pearl Harbor!"

At the organizational level, this "folklore" information is provided to help new employees fit in, to make sure new employees do not violate the behavior norms that have developed over time, and to strengthen the bonds among non-supervisory employees (the "us" that's got to survive the evil deeds of the managerial "them").

The more rigid the cultural boundaries established by folklore, the more hospitable the climate is for Theory X managers. As you recall, Theory X managers tend to favor rules, regulations, and other barriers to normal, human interaction. That's why Theory X survives like some malevolent virus, despite more than 50 years of research and evidence to support Theory Y management.

It's simply easier.

Easier, that is, for managers who want to maintain social distance from workers and don't want to have to deal with the facts of workers' lives and frustrations. It's easier just to say that results are all they care about. ("If these people can't do the work, let's get some people in here who can!")

Here is the important issue these people miss: Theory X is actually easier for workers. After all, they are free to do as little work as possible, and they don't have to bother with managerial relationships beyond what is needed to pick up on the manager's moods. Social distance works both ways.

Make no mistake, one of the first things workers learn in Theory X organizations is what the lowest level of effort is that will escape criticism. This becomes the *de facto* pace of work, and woe to any employee who breaks that norm and lets management know that more productivity is possible.

But what if the company provides rewards for outstanding performance? One employee, winner of several such awards, spoke privately with his manager. "Please don't give me any more awards," he asked. "I no longer have any friends here!"

Culture and peer pressure (culture's enforcement mechanism) often constrain intelligent action. Employees get caught between opposing choices: joining up with management, or sticking with their non-supervisory colleagues.

Make no mistake, being a Theory Y manager and getting workers to do what management wants is hard work. Would-be Theory Y managers need to consider a few things about the fundamentals of human behavior and the sociology of groups:

Three Fundamental Principles of Human Behavior

1. Behavior that is rewarded will be repeated, and behavior that is ignored or rebuked will be extinguished.

2. Groups can influence or control the behavior of their managers by withholding attention and not responding when unpopular subjects are discussed.

3. Getting groups of reluctant individuals to join up with management happens only as a result of a managerial strategy applied over time and with great patience.

This is why there are so few true Theory Y managers today, despite 50 years of manager training based on the works of such brilliant theorists as McGregor, Maslow, McClelland, Bennis, and Schein. If you are serious about the profession of management, check out these five exceptional theorists and contributors who have done so much to shape contemporary management practice.

Reader, you have a challenge and an opportunity: to overcome Theory X peer pressure and discipline yourself to be patient with people who are just responding to their own cultural imperatives. Can you give them time and support for the join-up process? Far too many managers choose not to make the effort.

Reinterpreting McGregor

Douglas McGregor drew the dividing line between authoritarian management as the management norm and employee participation as the management ideal. The either/or tenor of his proposition that Theory X is the opposite of Theory Y supports the interpretation by many consultants and academics that Theory X managers wear the black hats.

The Theory Y manager, conversely, has been positioned as a hero and the ideal manager: the man or woman who wears the white hat in the corporate combat between the quick, productive, and profitable employees and the reluctant, disinterested mass of workers.

This was a necessary differentiation. Consider the organizational culture in the 1950s when McGregor did his work. Essentially, all the managers were men, with the majority having served in the military during World War II or the Korean Conflict. Three major U.S. corporations employing approximately 110,000 employees each (IBM, the U.S. Department of Agriculture, and the U.S. Marine Corps) were, for all practical purposes, interchangeable in terms of their organization charts. To a surprising extent, theirs was a look-alike, think-alike, macho work culture. The Theory Y ideal was about as realistic as the dance of the sugarplum fairies—hardly the style of real men! This attitude was expressed many times over the years by managers who told me, in effect, "I don't want to waste my time and energy and attention on thanking people for doing what they're supposed to be doing anyway. If they get praise from me, it's going to be for something really big!"

McGregor's task was to highlight in bold relief the potential inherent in a research-based enlightened approach to dealing with workers, versus what was possible with the status quo.

Advocates of enlightened management held up Theory Y managers as paragons of interpersonal virtue. Such imagery was as polarizing in workplaces as the terms X and Y themselves. Managers who were trained to be open, caring, and inclusive when it came to making decisions were hired and then eventually subjected to intense peer pressure to abandon their so-called fuzzy ideas and ridiculous practices. Understandably, most did.

A participant in a sensitivity training program for managers wrote a thank-you note to me, not so much for the program, but for helping him realize that he would never be able to use the values he believed in in his corporate role. He explained that this was why he was leaving his company for a role in a religious organization. Other managers told me that they had been warned to *"enjoy the program, but don't expect to use what you learn"* when they returned to work. "Theory X 'rules,'" a high-level manager told me. "And no matter how much we want to be Theory Y guys, you can't do it one manager at a time."

Another View of Theory X

After years of rejection and repudiation, Theory X was given new respectability by academic and consultant Scott Parry. Parry's research led him to conclude that Theory Y doesn't work for everyone; some managers are so steeped in authoritarian experiences that they cannot stop giving orders, and feel compelled to maintain their social distance from employees.

This limits their ability to work effectively with groups that demand involvement, Parry maintains, but they still are valuable corporate assets.

There are some employees who, for a constellation of reasons, need the security and structure that comes from responding to orders. Their need to be responders rather than initiators limits their upward mobility, but such "good soldiers" are needed down in the ranks.

Realistically, there are some good guys among all those who appear to be Theory X managers, and there are some settings in which Theory X management is not only appropriate but necessary, such as in situations in which directions and orders must be given in order to maintain administrative and procedural discipline or to control finances or traffic, and in certain instructional/correctional settings. The growth of highly visible, politicized religious communities in the U.S. leads us to conclude that some Americans are demanding and even embracing dogmatic leaders who will work to create a counterforce within the larger society against the movement toward more inclusion, greater personal freedom, and critical examination and challenge of traditional beliefs.

18

To put conceptual handles on these realities, Parry borrowed from the work of Eric Berne and his enormously popular book, *Games People Play: The Psychology of Human Relations.* In that 1964 best seller, Berne introduced the idea that some relationships are based on essential parity (i.e., *I'm okay, you're okay*). He described these as adult-adult transactions, a definition that fits comfortably with Theory Y values that allow managers to see even direct reports as peers and colleagues in a common effort. ("I'm a responsible adult and you're a responsible adult; we just have different responsibilities.") [1]

In my experience, one of the greatest and most distressing failures to bring Theory Y management to a work setting occurred in Berkeley, California in the mid-1970s. Wesley Pomeroy, an acknowledged leader and innovator in law enforcement, was police chief from 1974 to 1977. He was defeated from within his own department by thugs with badges who did not want the reforms in personal responsibility and accountability that Pomeroy advocated. Sadly, the apologist-activists in that community did not support the man who most closely represented the ideals they claimed to believe in. Whoever heard, back then, of cops wearing blue blazers, instead of uniforms and guns in holsters? But that was probably one of the less-radical reforms he advocated.

Theory X is identified with Berne's characterization of superior-subordinate relationships as *I'm okay, you're not okay,* the classic parent-child relationship in which one person talks down to the other person or otherwise behaves as the knowledgeable adult dealing with an uninformed child. Parent-child is a demeaning relationship between two adults, McGregor explained, and it is the basis for Theory X: the manager must tell workers what to do and how to do it, because they are not capable of figuring it out for themselves. Parry's research suggested that there are at least two sides to Theory X: First, an *enabling and facilitating* side for people whose skills are minimal or who need hands-on instruction or have learned to be dependent at work. Second, a *judgmental and disparaging* side, where managers make comments to and about others (more in line with the original and limiting vision of Theory X).

Not everyone will respond to Theory Y and its invitation to responsible participation. Some people want the high structure and certainty of being told what to do and need close supervision. These are not "bad" people or "stupid" employees—they just need to be managed differently. They should be matched up with leaders who understand and respect their needs. The long-term goal might be to build independence as well as teamwork, but building worker trust and confidence in their leader has to come first.

In Parry's scheme and in my experience, Theory X managers can be kind, caring, and supportive, yet still provide structure. For risk-averse individuals who are practically immobilized at the idea of making a mistake or failing, the close supervision of a kindly Theory X manager will be just what the doctor ordered.

It is important in this discussion of management style to acknowledge that some people who are devoutly Theory Y and committed to adult-adult relationships are just not capable of providing the close supervision implicit in a parent-child relationship. Such people are not likely to go into teaching, and might only reluctantly become parents. Send a Theory X to the rescue!

Parry's work illuminated key issues in management style. He identified these competencies in his Managerial Assessment of Proficiency, bridging the gap between McGregor's research on the management styles that lead to more-effective organizations and those concrete steps that can be taken to achieve managerial proficiency.

> The competencies that lead to managerial success are keyed to specific managerial requirements.

There are many models describing managerial competencies. However, the one developed by Parry is keyed specifically to supporting Theory Y as the most appropriate management style in the majority of situations. The competencies he identified have been proved to lead to managerial success, and they are keyed to specific managerial requirements. They can be acquired through short-duration training (hours instead of weeks). We will highlight them in the pages that follow.

McGregor, Parry, and other leading researchers prove, repeatedly, that the Theory Y management style creates more productivity and profit than any other. Theory Y delivers, but it also demands much of those who want to achieve what it can deliver.

The following chapters are about what it takes to become a competent manager.

Chapter 4 Note

1. Berne, considered the father of Transactional Analysis, contributed substantially to our emerging understanding of the psycho-social dynamics in interpersonal transactions. Current studies on relationship-selling borrow heavily from Berne's work. *Games People Play* was reissued in paperback in 1978 and 1996.

Chapter 5

Developing Competence through Performance-Specific Feedback

Theory Y managers are the exception rather than the rule. Many managers have had thousands of dollars' worth of training in Theory Y methodology, yet they can't seem to make permanent changes in the way they manage employees. Here is what managers have to do if they want to convince their people that they are for real:

Managers have to really listen to direct reports.

They must solicit workers' opinions and input during problem-solving meetings.

Managers have to support, encourage, and appreciate worker achievement and results.

They must develop employees' skills, both in formal training programs and by delegating "stretching" assignments.

They have to give their employees leadership roles in meetings.

Managers need to let people know that they are important to the company. This will increase their self-respect and they will become more confident.

They must use the pronouns "we," "us," and "our" consistently.

When managers don't do these simple things because they say they don't have time, it hardly matters what Theory Y behaviors they do adopt, because workers have already concluded that all that corporate training money has been wasted. When the manager tries on other Theory Y behaviors and is ignored because the workers don't believe the manager really wants to change, those behaviors soon disappear. That sends a clear message that Theory Y principles aren't really rooted in the manager's mind or heart.

> Workers want to see proof over time that their manager really and truly wants to make things better.

When a manager is serious about establishing new working relationships and creating a Theory Y partnership, he or she will have to overcome many obstacles. One of the smartest moves a manager can make right away is to establish a comfortable, non-threatening, low-key style. The one thing every worker has in common, beyond being an employee, is knowledge of and experience with the group's work. This natural common denominator is a logical place to begin strengthening relationships and creating a management style that respects workers for what they know and what they contribute to the organization.

Communication Skills: Prerequisites for a Winning Management Style

No matter the setting, every conversation between a manager and a worker is essentially an exchange of information. Person A gives information in order to set up person B to provide information in return. The manner or tone used by A will predict, in large measure, the kind of response B makes. An angry or demanding opening by A will lead to a defensive or hostile response by B.

Good communicators usually begin a conversation or discussion in a way that makes the other party comfortable. Once a rhythm of easy exchanges is established, the manager can ask for more substantive information, such as "What do you think about the amount of work that this group puts out?"

Most people respond with something like, *"It's okay"* or *"It's as good as any other group."* An aggressive, in-your-face kind of worker, however, might respond with, "What is it you're *really* after?"

The Theory Y manager is likely to say something like "I think there are probably some things we could do to be more productive, but I'm not the only one with ideas about how we could improve. That's why I want to talk with each of you."

It might take three months, six months, or even longer for the work group to coalesce into the team you want, depending on the situation. The question you want to think about is this: Between now and that point in the future, will you get burned out with the effort, and revert to being the kind of low-expectations, Theory X manager they are used to?

Developing a winning management style is a long-term process; it will not be a quick fix. There will be no conversion experiences on the road to the project deadline. Have you got the patience? Will you give yourself and your group the time required? Persistence pays off.

Relationships Are Built on Shared Information

When employees are asked to participate in a discussion about work, one of the first things they want to know is what the manager is going to do with the information. They do not expect a positive outcome; in fact, they have learned to expect the worst: layoffs, downsizing, outsourcing in the U.S. or to a foreign company, or something equally drastic and threatening.

Make these personal meetings as informal as conditions allow. Do not close the office door—better yet, conduct the meeting in a lunchroom or other semi-public space. Anything that suggests secret proceedings or the possibility that employees will be put under pressure will increase their anxiety and mistrust. (Employees always feel threatened when they are told, "The boss wants to see you.")

Let's say the discussion is of an information-gathering nature: the manager wants to identify performance strengths and weaknesses in a team or work group by getting the perspectives of each member of the team. The manager should not take too long to report back to the workers on what he or she has learned or decided. Generally, it's best to provide team feedback within a week, with a follow-up meeting time announced at the end of each meeting. ("You'll get a report of the notes I took and the talks with others when we meet next Wednesday at four o'clock.") When information is being sought from more than one person, each person should be asked the same questions in the same order. The manager should take notes during and after each "interview" so all the details are recorded.

It's now the meeting time on Wednesday, and the manager proceeds to share the information he or she has collected. No one should see the information until it is presented. It is the property of the group, and the group must hear it first, from you.

The information shared at the meeting should focus on responses workers made to the questions that were asked privately (without identifying anyone). When group members are given typescripts of the manager's notes, they will recognize their own individual comments. If their own observations are accurately reported, they will be more likely to believe that other comments, too, are accurate.

The manager should give the group a few minutes to consider the information and to ask questions. He or she then sets a date for the next meeting to discuss the interview data "…because it would be unrealistic to ask you to discuss so much information when you haven't had an opportunity to go over it and discuss it among yourselves." Employees are usually surprised when their manager acknowledges and encourages them to do what they were going to do anyway!

And then the manager says something totally unexpected. "Now that you've seen this information, do I have your permission to share it with my boss?" For most employees, this will be the first time a leader has asked for their permission to do anything. It's a powerful moment.

Welcome to the World of Responsible Adults

Several things have just happened that reveal the management style of the person chairing the meeting:

He or she asked for their input and asked about the work they do.

He gave them a report on the information they provided.

He made copies for each member.

He asked them to prepare to discuss their information.

He set a definite time to discuss the information.

He asked for permission to share *their* data outside the group.

He conducted a short meeting without any theatrics.

He did not make editorial comments about the process or try to sell the process.

He treated them as adult colleagues, but made no demands on them to do anything beyond participating in the scheduled discussion.

No matter how biased people are for or against management, what this manager did certainly made an impression. The general attitude might still be to wait and see what happens next, but the manager got their attention.

Winning managers send clear messages:
Employees are adults.

There is no substitute for being treated like an adult. It's not that companies and institutions *intend* to reduce people to the status of big children, but the reality is that corporate life tends to do just that.

Winning managers send two clear messages:

Message 1: Employees are adults and will be treated like adults.

Message 2: Every member of the management team is also an employee of the organization.

> The major differences between workers and managers lie in the realm of roles and responsibilities.

What about Power and Authority?

In most work environments, the so-called power that managers are permitted to use is regulated through either government restriction (as in the case of arbitrary terminations) or by contractual agreement (i.e., limits on contracting or committing corporate funds).

One very bright, accomplished company president with 160 employees was taken aback by the suggestion that he is just another employee, and thus should treat *all* workers as equals. "If I treat employees that way, won't I lose my power?" Sadly, what he meant was, "Won't employees stop being afraid of me?"

> Power, authority, and the fear they invoke are the tools of Neanderthal managers.

A fearful employee tends to withhold information from the manager and other employees (which is not something any manager wants). Work environments should be energy-exchange systems. If there is a system malfunction, it will prevent early discovery of problems and effectively block opportunities for fast, cost-effective recoveries. Whether the problem is a human one or a mechanical one, it should be addressed and corrected as soon as possible, because the sooner it is recognized, the cheaper it is to fix. If employees are afraid of their manager, they won't go out of their way to be the bearer of bad news. Any system problem unattended to can force a system breakdown.

> The sooner a problem is recognized, the cheaper it is to fix.

Getting early-warning information from employees is a powerful payoff for a manager who has worked hard to develop a winning management style. When the work group comes together and coalesces itself into a team, members realize that the money they save by reducing re-work, break-downs, scrap, and lost time goes straight to the company's bottom line. Reducing costs creates profit—the best way to ensure job security for the group and its members.

About Developing Competence

In the United States Air Force, one senior enlisted person (a "crew chief") is assigned to each aircraft. It is the crew chief's responsibility to make sure that the aircraft meets all performance criteria (which can only happen when all mechanical and systems maintenance is performed as pre-scribed in the maintenance manuals). It's the crew chief's responsibility to release the aircraft to its pilot *only* when it is ready to perform the assigned mission.

It's not much of a stretch to think of managers as crew chiefs: after all, they must use a variety of skills and knowl-edge, as well as the most appropriate and effective manage-ment style, to get work groups ready to perform assigned tasks and to meet specific criteria regarding schedule, cost, and quality.

> It's the manager's responsibility to see that each individual is ready to perform as required.

The manager is expected to prepare each employee to do his or her job. Some workers will need more help than others. The manager coaches this one, praises that one, and chats with still another, being formal with some people and infor-mal with others. The manager always gives each person approximately equal time, however. No single management approach will fit everyone: the manager needs to connect with each employee in the way that works best for that individual. And don't forget that the behavior that gets rewarded gets repeated.

> **Management Tip:** Say *Please* when you ask some-one to do something, and say *Thank you* when the task is complete. These are signs of respect.

Another point about feedback: You are trying to develop competence in individual employees, but you cannot do this unless you have frequent conversations with individuals about their performance and their improvement targets. Don't restrict these conversations to those occasions when you must address performance deficiencies, such as the annual performance appraisal. A year is a long time to wait for feedback—too long to diagnose and correct deficiencies, and too long to be of any developmental help. No more than 90 days should go by without a formal, scheduled conversation about performance, contributions, and job satisfaction. To use an automotive analogy, no one who truly cares about their car or truck would even contemplate letting it go for an entire year without changing the oil and filter and periodically checking the tire pressure.

> How do you improve performance? By giving and receiving fast feedback on performance against targets.

A winning management style centers in large measure around the overall goal of helping workers succeed, reinforcing people when they do the right things correctly, and helping them derive more satisfaction from their jobs. Some of this nurturing needs to happen daily and weekly, but all of it certainly needs to be done every three months, *at the very least.*

Here's what I mean. Let's say a manager is having a quarterly meeting with an employee. "Sally," he says, "I think you would benefit from an improvement in your writing skills. Does that interest you?" The manager is providing feedback about a skill area in which improvement is needed, but his use of the word "benefit" suggests that if she improves these skills, it might make her eligible for better assignments, more pay, or even a promotion.

It's also the manager's job to call Sally's attention to her deficient writing skills, but it's up to Sally to take the initiative by asking what he recommends. The manager might agree to send Sally to a training course or to get the company to pay for an evening course.

He might tell her that it's something she needs to take care of on her own. The manager is saying that the choice is up to her. If company time and money are involved in her choice, however, the manager should follow up. There should be two-way feedback. Whatever the outcome, the manager should document his conversation with Sally about her performance.

People make choices every day. The obligation of a manager is to develop the group's workers—not to take over their professional development. Who knows? Sally might say, "I can't go to school at night because I'm in a bowling league." If that is the case, what should the manager say? "Okay, Sally, if that's your choice."

Why should a manager expend energy pushing Sally to do something from which she would benefit? Sally made a choice. Who's to say it wasn't the right choice for her at that time? A manager employing a winning management style will put his or her energy into individuals who want to improve *and* who will accept support and encouragement to do so.

This example illustrates one other distinction between Theory Y managers and Theory X managers:

> Theory Y managers recognize that adults make choices, and that other people have to accept the fact that those choices are the result of decisions made by competent adults.

The manager might disagree with or even disapprove of an employee's decision, but to stay in the adult-adult transactional mode, the manager must respect the other person's right to choose, regardless of the consequences. If this sounds strange or runs contrary to what you have experienced, here is something that will be even more unusual: Theory Y managers do not motivate individuals! Instead, they create situations in which individuals make decisions that are good for them, for their team, and for the company. So don't hire anyone you will have to motivate!

A View of Management Styles

One of the most popular management styles discussed in training courses during the post-McGregor period showed how a manager might move from an authoritarian management style to a participative management style. It looked like this:

Tell ——— Sell ——— Consult ———Join

On the authoritarian end of the continuum, people are told what to do. If the manager has been to charm school and has discovered that people don't like to receive orders, he might try to sell them on the need to do things, maybe conjuring up some so-called benefits to doing the work. These are both Theory X approaches: people must be told what to do or seduced into doing it. On the other end of the continuum, employees get a greater share of decision-making prerogative in that they are consulted or actually asked to sit down with the manager to make a decision. In some instances, the manager actually delegates decisions to workers (perhaps when vacation schedules must be negotiated, or when employee preferences should be given some consideration.

With the exception of the **sell** position (which is dishonest), Tell, Consult, and Join are all legitimate management style options. In an emergency, even an ardent Theory Y manager might tell someone what to do or give orders.

But the important point in digging up this old model is to consider this question: *What are the long-term implications or consequences of using any of these styles on a consistent basis?* What do people learn about their manager? What do people learn about themselves? In what directions do people grow? How do they feel about themselves? And does any of this relate to performance and profitability?

The answers to these questions probably justify the attention being paid to management style. Look at the model again. There is a lot of organizational intelligence in it.

Giving Situation-Specific Feedback

It's not enough to say, *"You're doing a great job, Bill!"* Think about it: What does "great" mean? Practically nothing—or almost anything. Generally, employees understand the comment to mean that Bill is not giving the manager any trouble. He keeps his mouth shut and does what he's supposed to do. The manager could make that comment without ever observing Bill's performance, so is it really feedback?

What Bill wants and what every other employee wants as well is to be recognized for really good performance, and to be acknowledged for the *specific* things they do that make or made a difference. It's one of the easiest things a manager can do, and it doesn't cost a cent. Here's what I mean:

At a staff meeting or a coffee break, the manager can say something like, "Hey, everybody! Bill saved this company almost $23,000 this morning when he picked up a billing error that was several months old. ABC owes us an additional 23 big ones, and that's going to look good on our monthly financials. *Thank you, Bill!*"

Bill probably earned half his annual salary with that discovery. Sure, he does a good job all the time, but in this instance, he created *significant value* through his diligence. He's pleased that his performance is being recognized, but it goes further than that: his colleagues know that their manager is watching and paying attention to *their* performance, too. No doubt about it, the manager wants more of that type of diligent performance, and is sure to notice and praise it when it happens.

Praise is a powerful tool, often producing unexpected second- and third-order benefits. Praising an individual's performance increases the likelihood that the manager will have a useful conversation about other abilities the individual can bring to the group's work.

Suppose the manager sits down with Bill to follow up. "What other kinds of interesting or curious things have you found in going over those accounts?" he asks. Perhaps Bill *has* found other anomalies that might lead to significant savings if they're looked into, but if no one asks him about his impressions or suspicions, he is not likely to volunteer that information.

> Praising an individual's performance leads to the discovery of other abilities the individual can bring to the group's work.

Pay attention to this: Why should any employee undertake extra effort when it isn't likely to be appreciated or even acknowledged? There is no way to calculate the power of job-specific praise in achieving performance improvements across an entire team, but everyone knows that even a little bit of praise goes a long way. Adopt a winning management style and you won't regret it.

Suppose the team is already good and everyone knows it? In the global economy where entire industries disappear for a while and re-emerge in China or India, is performance ever good enough? Never!

A winning management style can be used to keep work groups performing against targets that are increasingly precise in terms of deliverables. Here's what I mean:

Let's say you trying to reduce the company's manufacturing costs so you can reduce a product's purchase price. As soon as the numbers go down significantly, news comes that a competitor is now producing the same quality for less, and another has adopted new technology in manufacturing plants. What would you do? Today's performance targets are targets-in-transition and you must be prepared to motivate your people to reach targets that are constantly being moved. It's said that the Japanese won the car market because of variations in the diameter and weight of pistons. In American engines, with piston variances up to five times greater than those accepted by the Japanese, more horsepower, RPMs, and fuel are required to mask the vibrations of unbalanced pistons. As a result, U.S.-made engines (and vehicles) self-destruct at a comparatively accelerated rate. Perhaps a few targets should have been changed...

In a busy corporate or industrial environment, there are a lot of details to monitor and control. How much easier these tasks become when the manager has a workforce composed of individuals and teams who *also* look and listen and care about results. Another payoff of a winning management style.

Chapter 6

Building Respect for Self, Team, and Company

Management is the manipulation of variables, some of which are people, for the goal-directed release of energy toward cost-effective results.

If this definition is acceptable, then it's obvious that there's more to the manager's job than winning friends and influencing people. If a manager cannot win with people, however, he or she had better be a truly exceptional performer.

It has been said about the late U.S. Navy Admiral Hyman Rickover, widely regarded as the father of the nuclear submarine, that there have been few people in positions of command who exhibited a more disagreeable management style. Rickover, however, was possessed of a powerful vision, and was extremely effective at turning his vision into a reality. That's why he was able to recruit so many capable officers, and why he was permitted to fend off retirement from the Navy until he was in his 80s.

But for managers who don't go on visionary quests or who are not gifted with an exceptionally high IQ, a querulous management style will spell career disaster. Such managers move through the organization leaving a wake of ill feelings and bad energy. They acquire reputations for being more trouble than they are worth. In a turn-around or salvage operation, such behavior might be excusable—but not in the average work environment.

So, it comes down to this: Managers have to get workers to perform at higher levels than ever before, and have to do that without creating alienation and sparking retaliation. It will take a lot of patience, but also a solid understanding of the basics of change management.

In Times of Change...

In situations in which change is inevitable, every individual will feel some degree of threat to their jobs and their egos. When it comes to job security, keep in mind the new reality: there are few tasks (if any) that cannot be subcontracted or outsourced. Most workers now recognize this.

As for ego and self-concept, everyone will have private moments when they doubt themselves and wake up in the middle of the night with worry. *Am I good enough to be retained?* Older workers have another concern. *Will they replace me with some kid one-third my age and at one-third my salary?* Operational managers with the right management style can influence how employees deal with the stress of change (and even the possibility of change).

These are real issues that no manager working below the executive level is likely to be able to influence. But what operational managers *can* influence is how their employees deal with the stress of change—if they adopt the right management style. Ultimately, it comes down to how people feel about themselves.

Effective Management in Times of Change

The effective manager tells workers the truth about the nature and scope of changes being proposed, to the extent that he or she knows it.

If jobs within the group are threatened, the manager discusses options/opportunities elsewhere in the company.

The manager explains possible changes to his or her role.

The manager encourages workers to contribute to a "win" for everyone by staying at their tasks and keeping their productivity up.

Of course, these same four things should also be done if there is a change in management because of corporate acquisition or reorganization, or when key individuals are promoted or transferred and new managers take over.

A winning management style makes for an easier transition for workers, as well as for their newly arrived manager. It communicates quickly who the manager is and what he or she wants employees to do. You see, deep down, *every employee wants to please the manager,* and that requires clarity about the manager's expectations.

Operational managers with the right management style can influence how employees deal with the stress of change.

41

Building Self-Respect and Self-Esteem

When managers understand that people in subordinate relationships want to please their bosses, it opens up an entire world of opportunities to move them toward exceptional performance. It's not "manipulative" in the usual, negative sense of the word. Instead, it's simply putting a very human need or desire to good purpose, for the benefit of the organization *and* the individual.

Here's what I mean: Let's say Sally turns in a report. Instead of just accepting it with a nod of acknowledgement, the manager holds the report, really looking at it, and then says something like, "This looks great, Sally. It really pleases me to receive such work. I look forward to reading it!"

What does that require on the part of the manager? Two things:

About 30 seconds to focus on this one individual.

An understanding of the power (yes, the POWER) he or she has to tell this employee *You have done well, and I am pleased!*

But what if the report isn't perfect? Then the manager says something like, "Oops! There's a typo on the cover. Sally, could you fix that and then let me have it? I will be pleased to read it then." Oops! is a comment without judgment, criticism, or rebuke. It's not the end of the world, and no great catastrophe. Sally corrects the typo and returns the document. The manager says something like, "Thanks, Sally. Thanks for the quick turnaround. I look forward to reading it."

Such an exchange might carry emotional messages, such as…

My boss made eye contact with me.

He accepts me, even if I made a mistake.

He appreciates my efforts to do good work.

He makes me feel good about myself when he could have made me feel bad or not okay.

I will make extra efforts to please this manager!

Here's another example of how you can build self-esteem: Suppose Joe is making an interim report at a project meeting on work-in-place and funds expended-to-date. Basic stuff. Nothing sexy. So the manager is presented with a choice:

Option #1: To say, "Okay, Joe. Thanks."

Option #2: "It's always good news to hear that work is getting done faster than money is being spent. Thanks, Joe, for the report."

In Option #2, Joe is being told that he and those whom he represents are doing well, and that their efforts are appreciated. In a roomful of people, Joe is also "on stage" for an extra minute or two, and he's being praised.

But suppose Joe's report isn't so positive? The manager can give Joe the same positive reinforcement by asking, "Joe, what are the chances you and the others can catch up on the work and find some ways to get control of the budget?" Again, no rebuke or critique. Instead, one professional is asking another how they can both overcome the glitch. After Joe explains the recovery plan, the manager is given another opportunity to say something positive: "That sounds like good headwork, Joe. Please keep me posted." What these examples illustrate is the point of this book:

> Building and *communicating* a winning management style means trying to build self-esteem, self-respect, and pride in every conversation with every employee.

It's easy to do. The difficulty, if there is one, is to get managers new to this process to make it a habit to build people up at every opportunity—to make it part of their daily existence.

It's not false, phony, or baloney. It is a proven way to win with people. The book *How to Win Friends and Influence People* is older than anyone reading this one, but Dale Carnegie's message from 1936 is still true:

> To win with people, you have to make them feel good about themselves and feel good about collaborating with you.

This is the essence of the winning management style.

These examples are not meant to be simplistic, and I'm not trying to paint the manager as some kind of Pollyanna. I offer them because they all are based on the logic of street transactions: You help me get mine, and I'll help you get yours.

The workplace is the most stable environment in many people's lives. This is reality. People come to work from all kinds of distressing home circumstances. When a manager makes people feel good about themselves and the work they are doing, and then takes a minute or two now and then to speak to them as equals (*I'm okay, you're okay*: adult-to-adult), there is a transaction in process that pays dividends way beyond any reasonable expectations.

The bonds that are formed from these kinds of simple interactions will probably never be spoken of, but the manager who creates them with most or all of his or her direct reports will never fail. He/she will receive too much support and loyalty from too many people for that to happen.

Douglas McGregor told this same story when he created Theory X and Theory Y. Eric Berne wrote a book about the power of these transactions in everyday life. Scott Parry created the Managerial Assessment of Proficiency (MAP) to help leaders develop competence as managers. This book focuses on the simple things managers can do on the way to creating a winning management style.

Building Respect within the Team

Allegiances within the workplace must go beyond managers and individual employees. We don't feel positive about others until we first feel good about ourselves. This is why it's so important for managers to help workers develop self-respect and self-esteem. Boosting everyone's ego, however, can sometimes backfire if you end up with a lot of people with big egos who have trouble working together. But this, too, can be handled by a thoughtful manager who has developed a winning management style.

Process check: What is this book about? Among all these tales of virtuous managerial deeds, it's possible to lose sight of the fact that the purpose of the book is to show managers how to focus on cost-effective performance that helps them achieve specific, measurable targets. It is also intended to point out those small courtesies and explicit ways of communicating that allow employees to see their manager demonstrating a management style that is pleasing to them.

No manager succeeds alone (but many self-destruct, all by themselves). Next to being a close relative of a senior executive, the best job-security protection a manager can have is a strong, competent team committed to the success of everyone on the team, including the manager. The best way to get that protection is to be a manager with a winning management style.

Those who have been in the military learn that there is no plan of man or God that cannot be caused to fail by a corporal and two privates. Low-status people can corrupt the best strategies if they feel a need or have a reason to do so. In such instances, the manager may *know* he was sabotaged, but will be unable to prove it.

Such games go on all the time in business organizations, too. They are a waste of energy, resources, and the manager's credibility, and they create mistrust among people who should behave like colleagues. There has to be a "we" feeling at work if people are to perform successfully. Creating that feeling is a big part of the manager's role.

Erik Berne wrote a book in 1961 that was popular in the medical community: *Transactional Analysis in Psychotherapy.* Some insightful editor encouraged Berne to develop a version for the non-medical community, and *Games People*

Play became a best seller. After all, what's more basic than analyzing human interactions? What we learn from such books is how to anticipate and avoid unhappy transactions, and to understand the dynamics that underlie them.

Isn't the essence of being an effective manager a matter of setting the stage for winning transactions?

Start by being inclusive, because inclusiveness is key. As the manager thinks ahead, is he/she thinking *we?* Or *me?* A winning management style requires a "we" perspective: you have to include and involve your people in every team or staff meeting, in every transaction.

A decision that everyone understands *and* agrees with is a good decision. Managers are always asking employees if they "understand." Of course they understand! The question they should ask instead is this one: Do the people who have to do the work, expend the energy, and work overtime to implement the actions *agree* with the decision?

It's unrealistic to think that employees will expend their best efforts to accomplish something they don't agree with or don't believe in, but everyday, people are asked to do work when they are not invested in the outcome.

> A winning management style requires a "we" perspective: you have to include and involve your people in every team or staff meeting, in every transaction.

Yes, I am talking about employees investing in the outcome. Some of their thinking and some of their ideas should be considered in every decision that they must implement.

Even the most dutiful employee wants more than to be an extension of the manager's will. It doesn't cost much for a manager to discuss things with employees before making a decision that involves them. "It seems like what we need to do is XYZ. What do you think? Is that the best way we can proceed? Do you have any suggestions?"

As obvious as these practices seem here, it is profoundly difficult for some people to yield to the intelligence of people they consider to be organizationally "inferior." Subordinates, people who earn less, people who don't have a university degree, people who are new or inexperienced, people who are impossibly young. Don't shut them out! One senior manager realized that he was doing just that—excluding others from participating in decisions. "My God, I not only do that at work, I do it to my kids at home every day!"

Actually, Douglas McGregor and other advocates of participative management never suggested that the newest, greenest employee should sit down with the company president to make decisions. However, when decisions affect the work done or the equipment used by people down in the organization, it makes sense to involve them in the decision-making process. After all, they are subject matter experts on the tasks they perform and the equipment they use. They all are capable of suggesting better, faster, cheaper ways to do what they do. All you have to do is ask.

> Collaborative decisions are generally better than the decisions of the most capable individual.

Savvy managers understand that decision making is a responsibility, not an individual prerogative. There is a lot of evidence from training programs and real work settings that collaborative decisions are better, generally, than the decisions of the most capable individual. And even if decisions aren't technically better, there is more group energy vectored toward making them work.

Also, there is an opportunity for team members to grow in their appreciation of the skills, experience, and contributions of others that otherwise might never become obvious. "We" is a powerful energizer of groups and individuals. If the manager does not involve workers, he demonstrates that he does not believe he is part of the "we." And if that's the case, it soon becomes "us against him and them," every time.

Building Respect for the Company

The manager might be considered "the company" to those who report to him/her, but the company is a living entity, too. It deserves the respect and support of its employees, but in these cynical times, some people think it's "cool" to disparage decisions and the people who make them.

It's bad form to bite the hand that feeds you, but it also destroys the social fabric that holds an organization together. Imagine the loss of respect a manager suffers in the eyes of executives when condescending remarks from his/her team get repeated up the line. It happens.

Good leaders understand the importance of confronting individuals who make anti-company comments—not only to rebuke, but to ask why. What do you hope to accomplish? How do you think it makes others feel? How do you think it makes *me* feel? Do you want to be associated with these kinds of comments? Do you think there is a long-term future for you here if such comments are identified with you? If you're unhappy here, why don't you let me help you with your résumé?

What is tolerated is validated. Basically going along to get along is NOT part of a winning management style. To the contrary: A winning management style is about setting and maintaining standards of conduct, as well as standards of performance. When everyone focuses on missions and profits, there is little need for social policing. Establish guidelines right away and ease up at that point in a group's development when people feel part of a tight and self-respecting team.

Some things are *not* okay—not because they violate some puritanical norms, but instead because they do not help individuals feel good about themselves, about their co-workers, and about the company (toward whose success everyone should be actively committed). Sexist and racist comments can have legal consequences. So can profanity; any pattern of demeaning remarks can be construed as harassment. This is the stuff of career death, but more importantly, these things sabotage all the efforts you and the team are making to build respect and cohesiveness.

A winning management style is about setting and maintaining standards of conduct, as well as standards of performance.

Managers with winning management styles send out positive messages: I am proud of my company. I like my job. I am proud of my co-workers and what we accomplish together. Alert managers actually do more than simply send out positive personal messages. They make copies of business news reports about the company and distribute them to employees so that everyone on the team knows the company's economic performance and its standing among competitors. Each employee should be equipped to build the company's reputation with people in the community.

Chapter 7

Redefining Roles and Responsibilities

When a manager starts to create opportunities for employees to have greater success and continue to make greater contributions, even minor changes will have an effect on people. It's not always possible to see the task-based social structure within which employees operate, but there is a web of interdependencies.

Most institutions get organized around **functions** (marketing, sales, finance, design, manufacturing, etc.). Functions, in turn, get subdivided into areas of similar tasks, led by people in **roles** designed to maintain organizational integrity (international marketing, domestic market development, etc.). Roles, in turn, are really defined by the **responsibilities** to be met by the individual in the role. Further, dividing lines between and among functions and roles are to be found where one set of responsibilities ends and another begins. Ideally, there should be no overlaps or confusion.

Operationally, however, precise definitions of functions, roles, and responsibilities blur over time. A strong sales manager intrudes on the territory of the marketing manager, and the manager of design wakes up one morning to find that the production manager has become the *de facto* design manager.

There's usually going to be some confusion along those boundary lines. Former colleague Dick Horrworth was once associated with a consulting firm called the Managerial Responsibility Guidance Corporation. They specialized in using interview protocols to find areas where there was confusion regarding managerial roles and responsibilities. The system the firm used had six levels of responsibility, from total to zero, based on the premise that when two or more individuals or groups think of themselves as having the same levels of responsibility for anything, things will fall through the cracks. Confusion leads to failure, and failure is expensive.

That dynamic assumption of responsibilities does not seem to work when the content of those jobs has remained unchanged for years, such as is often the case with salaried workers and the white-collar professionals whose jobs have always existed. Two employees of a bank situated in a rural community I worked in sat every afternoon recording the day's transactions in a ledger—two years after the entire system had been automated. Two years!

All Tasks Must Be Performed Satisfactorily

The focus in corporations and work groups within them is NOT supposed to be on who does which jobs, but rather on how to make sure that all the necessary tasks are performed. Managers need to modify work patterns so that the workers who have the right skills and the inclination to best perform certain tasks are allowed to do so.

The reality is that no one is competent in performing all tasks. While work can be assigned as the manager chooses, the best Theory Y managers use sensitivity and discretion when it comes to separating people from tasks they think they perform well. If there is only nominal competence, the work is probably accomplished with a lot of excess effort. Interpersonal skills and respect for the worker (adult to adult) come in handy if you have to shift responsibilities and people.

A word about position and job descriptions seems appropriate here. In many organizations, such descriptions are used mostly to establish a point in a salary range, rather than to accurately describe tasks and duties. Understandably, individuals are sometimes placed in roles that do not take advantage of their strengths, or for which they are not prepared.

A **job** is a collection of tasks and duties. It is assumed that anyone who can perform some tasks satisfactorily will also perform others equally well, but this is not a logical assumption, and it has led to a lot of failures among new hires and promotions. In the wooden-headed logic associated with bureaucracies, the decision to promote comes down to "fully satisfactory" performance or failure. To prevent failure, people often are sent to training programs simply to acquire skills to perform some element of their jobs at a satisfactory level.

Training is indeed an important adjunct to the American enterprise system. It is also a large industry that provides many useful services. But hidden among all its contributions is a fact of life: If one is 35 years old and does not write well (and consequently has never liked writing), how much difference will be made by forced participation in a 40-hour course on how to write reports?

But suppose that individual is great at dealing with subcontractors or developing plans for commercial projects. Think how much more benefit will be gained by using training time and budget for a course on contract negotiation to *build on strengths* instead of trying to overcome weaknesses.

Let someone else do the writing. Or the accounting. Or the customer service call-backs. Again, the important issue is to make sure that all tasks are performed well, not to insist that they be performed by someone in a specific role.

Can your HR department handle this revision of task responsibilities? You won't know until you ask. Your chances of getting it done are better if you develop the documentation for them, following the forms and formats they have to use. (Otherwise, they are almost guaranteed to say no.)

That Includes the Manager's Role, Too

A savvy manager will not be long in discovering which individuals have skills that are not being used in their roles. Where there are skills, there usually is pleasure in using them. Why not let those who have the skills the work group needs use them? Why not shift some responsibilities and duties within the group, so people can do more of what they like to do and do well? Do it on a trial basis, and see how things go.

Every managerial role is full of responsibilities and ill-defined tasks that require time and effort. When a manager's job is analyzed, many elements of the job turn out to be things that the manager is not required to do personally. Pass those elements along to staff who will do them well and enjoy doing them, develop new capabilities and experiences for their résumés, and find themselves more involved in the life of the work group.

With the probable exception of areas requiring confidentiality, any part of the manager's job can be subcontracted or delegated to members of the work group. The more tasks the manager can delegate, the more time he/she has to coach, counsel, think, plan, and develop staff competencies.

This makes so much sense that it ought to be routine practice, but it isn't routine in most organizations. The excuses range from *"They" won't allow* it or *The staff doesn't want to do more work,* to *supervising delegated work takes too much time.*

But reason #1 is that the *manager* is supposed to make sure that things are done correctly.

This is a control issue. Individuals don't get selected to be managers unless they have demonstrated the ability to get in control and stay in control of work and people who perform it. Nevertheless, over-control is a flaw in many systems and in many individuals.

Every winning manager is given a certain amount of latitude when it comes to developmental opportunities, but being "in control" and allowing people to learn and grow appear to be mutually exclusive ideas, don't they?

Consider this: The most-effective control is fast feedback on performance. That means touching base with people responsible for tasks *while there is still time to ensure success!*

Notice that I said "ensure success" rather than "prevent failure." It is an important distinction. One is very positive and the other is essentially negative and demeaning, reflecting a judgmental "parent" overseeing a mistrusted "child." Hardly a way to build a positive relationship, is it? How a manager "sees" and thinks is important.

For many managers, maintaining a healthy sense of control is a major personal challenge. Keep in mind that a strong need for control is generally rooted in personal insecurity and a fundamental mistrust of people in general and employees and colleagues in particular. If you want to be a good manager—and a winning one—read what the experts say about power and control, particularly the views of those who advocate participative management.

I remember visiting the home of a newly consecrated Episcopal bishop and asking him why he thought he was chosen for the role from a dozen other candidates. His answer was candid and surprising. "It's not because I was a better priest than the others. It's because I organized a fund-raising campaign that raised six million dollars. But I didn't raise the money. That was done by a relatively new parishioner. He, more than anyone or anything else, won me this amazing honor."

Remember, all this emphasis on creating a winning management style is about building a work group or team that will make you look good as a manager and as a people-developer. If you and your employees make that kind of contract, why would they let you down? And if that's not enough reassurance, consider this: You never know which one of them is going to do the very thing that will get your promoted!

Chapter 8

Rewarding and Promoting

The trend toward creating flat organizations will continue. There will be no return to the many-layered organization of yesteryear, with its stacks of supervisors supervising supervisors and executives at a far remove from the organization's work. Gone, too, is the almost endless upward mobility for those who are able to advance repeatedly through company training or schooling on their own or through equal opportunity initiatives.

Ah, the good old days. The opportunities are now largely horizontal, not vertical. Pay differentials, if any, are not likely to be enough to purchase that new SUV.

The managers with winning managerial styles know this. They also know that for most employees, money is not a prime motivator; employees who can make significantly more money elsewhere will leave to do so. The tired lament of *give us more money and we'll do more work* is as empty as it ever was. It's just a way to tell the manager who is not free to give them more money that he/she is as impotent as the workers feel themselves to be.

Work has always been a trade-off: time, talent, and effort in exchange for money and other considerations. When money is not negotiable, other considerations become very important (perks, bonuses, profit-sharing, for example). Most organizations have a system of awards and rewards, but this is usually tied to a manager's ability and willingness to document the performance that is worthy of recognition. This leads us to discussion of a weakness in too many managers: lousy documentation.

The Mysterious "They" and "Them"

Employees are usually aware of the company's reward system and what it takes to earn them an award or bonus, but they get discouraged and demotivated when they discover that the system is deeply flawed, if not dishonest. The flaw I'm referring to is a particularly reprehensible one: Worthy individuals most often do not receive awards, because their managers fail to present documentation that is credible to an awards committee! In most cases, people on such committees do not know the individuals, and might not have ever visited the work site.

Every organization has its own required forms and formats for distribution of funds, personnel actions, or awards. Managers who do not bother to study the forms and try to understand the information and supporting documentation they require are lazy or sloppy, and the employees lose out on important recognition.

But long before it gets to that point, every manager should be documenting the specifics of employee behavior, positive or negative. That's not the prevailing attitude, however. Many managers rationalize their failure to keep good employee records: It's not easy to fire people (particularly in larger organizations), and if you can't get people fired, why collect the documentation required for removal? When managers look at the payroll and see the names of employees with dreadful reputations for non-performance, they think, *See? They won't fire people, no matter how sorry their performance!* If you want to terminate an employee, you have to document specific information relative to their performance.

What kind of documentation are we talking about? The same kind of information on good performance as for poor performance: A signed note with a time and date, and the names of any others involved. Any scheduled meeting, even if it was conducted in an informal setting, should be documented. Individual improvements should be noted, and plans for performance improvements should be recorded for follow-up. This takes minutes!

Then, every single day, make notes on every employee who does something noteworthy. Make a note of it on a computer, or dictate it for later entry into individual files. How long does that take?

If a manager submits a documented history of steady improvement and anecdotal notes about exceptional performance on a number of specific occasions, the awards committee is likely to approve the manager's request to give that employee a reward or award. Then the manager won't have to say, sadly (because he, too, was turned down), "They just wouldn't buy it. Maybe next time?" Employees won't buy it, either. You have the power to change that.

Finding Advancement in a Flat Organization

A lot of organizational phenomena are explained by referring to Pareto's Law, which says that the world is divided 80/20: 20 percent of the people do 80 percent of the work and make 80 percent of the money. Another 20 percent of the people cause 80 percent of the trouble managers and society must resolve.

One in five workers sounds like a generous ratio of achievers. Perhaps it's more like 5 percent, or 1 in 20—but surely *someone* within every work group can be developed for advancement or for some kind of leadership role. *Developed* is the operational word. The organization needs in-house expertise and long-time employees who commit to its success. Employee development benefits the individual and the organization. Developed through the attention of the manager. Developed through expanded responsibilities, opportunities to perform other tasks, and maybe even a rotation to another work group.

Against the background of pressure on everyone to hit the numbers, it's pretty easy to overlook this gift of opportunity to the individual and to the company.

In a way it is "favoritism," so the manager had better have a justifiable reason (other than a personal relationship with the chosen person) to develop and advance an individual. There will be some resentment if it is not understood why a particular individual has been singled out to grow beyond them and the work they do. The manager needs to tell them, openly and without apology. Suppose the manager says something like this:

"You all have noticed that Bill is getting some special assignments and that he is frequently meeting with me and working a lot of overtime. You may also know that Bill has being going to school at night for six years, and will complete work on his degree in business administration by Christmas. I think there's a chance Bill can get promoted if he gets additional work experience here, so I hope you will support Bill—and me—in seeing if we can open the door for him."

When an opportunity comes to help someone in a way that no one else can, act on it. Do it! It's really the only way you can repay the people who have helped *you* get where *you* are.

The Manager as Mentor

Most people who advance in organizations do so, in part, because they had a mentor. Or several. A *mentor* is a senior person who recognizes something in those individuals and decides to coach them, advise them, and talk with them about how to perform and get noticed. Such advice is invaluable.

Mentoring does not appear in job descriptions. People with a winning management style are mentors by nature. It's something they need to do—to help others and perhaps pass along favors done for them by mentors in the past. Long ago in my own professional life, I had a mentor who used to say to me, "If you're not contributing to the success of those around you, you're wasting your life!" He was right on the money.

But even those managers who are driven to be mentors learn, early on, that Pareto's Law works. There are only a few individuals in any population with the diligence and discipline to take advantage of a mentor's efforts.

Whether it's 1 in 20 or 1 in 5, the majority of people (some very competent and very nice) have priorities other than advancement within the organization. Wish them well and back away. No need to slam the door; most will never come back to ask for help if they rejected it when it was first offered.

Another thing about mentors, in the true Theory Y tradition, is that they can occasionally be harsh and demanding and unsympathetic, and intolerant about excuses. This tends to be a weakness, even in managers who possess other elements of a winning management style. To be fair, there are just some people who cannot be reached with subtlety. Motivational guru Frederick Herzberg referred to them as people who need a dose of *KITA*—a kick in the *attitude*.[1]

Being a mentor is a limited responsibility. If it were ever reduced to words, the contract between a mentor and the person to be helped might read something like this:

> I see in you abilities that can be developed. I am willing to help you develop those abilities, but your desire for my help must be as strong as my need to help you.

> I am helping you because it's the right thing to do. When you quit doing what I tell you to do, I quit being your mentor. After all, we're both volunteers.

Remember, pages ago, when I spoke of the manager who offered Sally an opportunity to advance? She turned it down, and he backed off. Why should a manager quit when someone has talent and unused abilities, and might be promotable? Because you are dealing with adults. They should not be persuaded, cajoled, or conned. Just give them a choice, and let them decide. Never argue with an adult over his/her choices, and never repeat the same offer. (If this sounds arbitrary, remember that you're seeing it in a *guide*. But consider it anyway.)

In my experience as a mentor, I came to realize that the largest part of the process is planting the idea that the individual being coached has potential outside his or her present role or direction. Some people just can't see themselves doing something different from what they have done before—something outside their envelope of experience. You might have to persist with the suggestion over some months. I know a young woman with an MBA who was working as a placement specialist and teaching HR courses on the weekends and evenings. I planted the idea that she could succeed in sales, earning more and gaining more job satisfaction. She decided to quit the placement job and become a freelance consultant, which I encouraged. But I also suggested that she talk to a friend of mine who was looking for someone to sell advertising for a new men's magazine. To cut to the chase, she is making more money than she imagined and having more fun, and she has developed a course in successful selling, based on her new experiences.

I was once locked into adversarial relationships with consultants who considered me an interloper because I was new to their team and was critical of some of their strategies. They had me effectively isolated, so I asked a bright intern to interview my primary antagonist, explaining that she was working on a research project. The young man was so engaging and so popular that he was able to elicit the information I was not being given. As a result, I improved my position, and in the process, the young man discovered abilities that led him in an unexpectedly new direction. He is now, ten years later, a partner in a major international consulting firm.

What personal qualities make a good mentor? I will share the ones that get my attention: Bright-eyed intelligence. Curiosity. Willingness to consider new information without becoming defensive. Energy. Discipline. Interpersonal skill. Willingness to engage in conversation, and the courage to disagree. And a desire to see others shine.

One word of caution: Don't get emotionally involved. The people you choose to mentor are free agents, and they might reject your help. Maybe you are wrong in your assessment of them. Perhaps you want them to succeed more than they want it for themselves. You might think that their reasoning is deeply flawed, but remember that it's their choice. You must respect that. If so, wish them well and assure them that you respect their decision. Then move on.

With a winning management style, you learn the boundaries between direction and control, between help and domination, between legitimate managerial responsibilities and intrusions into the personal space of others. When these boundary lines become clear, the manager's job will become much easier. And you'll have more fun.

Chapter 8 Note

1. Herzberg's research on motivation is some of the most controversial you will come across, but the findings of his research have been proved through more than 10,000 replications of the model in many different cultural settings. Don't fail to check him out.

Chapter 9

As the Running Shoe People Say…

Researchers tell us that there are twenty-one chief attributes or behaviors associated with a winning management style, based on the experiences of thousands of effective managers. Top managers use these behaviors 24/7—not just when they go to work. These behaviors are rooted in their overall attitude toward other people.

Winning Managerial Behaviors

Treat each person with respect.

Do not speak as though people don't know their job.

Ask for their opinion about work issues.

Say "Please" and "Thank you."

Express appreciation for work done well and on time.

Let people know about training courses that might be good for them.

Be willing to admit your mistakes.

Never rebuke people for errors (especially not in public!).

Focus on solutions, instead of looking for someone to blame.

Notice when people are stressed or having problems at work or home.

Be sensitive and supportive when people have family problems.

Compliment people every chance you get (appearance, achievement, attitude, etc.). Just be sincere.

Coach people who are having trouble with a task.

When overtime is necessary, you be there, too.

Be willing to acknowledge and reward outstanding performance.

Be willing to stand up for capable individuals when promotions are possible.

Remain open to suggestions regarding changes or improvements in office or plant processes.

Work as hard as everyone else.

Demonstrate your pleasure in working with your employees.

Infuse the work group with confidence to excel.

Help people decide whether or not to leave the organization if they cannot seem to meet performance standards.

If you do not yet do these things, you have some learning objectives to meet. In the meantime, check your core beliefs. You are well on your way to becoming a Theory Y manager if you believe in the principles that follow:

Theory Y management holds that:

1. Most people are honest and will not cheat you.

2. People make mistakes, and they should not be punished.

3. Anger is counterproductive.

4. You can help people be successful at work.

5. Yours is the "voice" of the company, and you should represent a high standard in personal conduct.

6. Your team will not let you fail if they see you supporting others.

7. You are not the only smart person in the group, nor the one with the most-relevant experience in every situation.

8. Allowing your direct reports to participate in the decision-making process does not weaken you as the designated manager.

9. Work is more satisfying when everyone is involved in setting performance targets, and when everyone works together to achieve or surpass those targets.

10. When you contribute to the success of others, you will always be a winner. (This is perhaps the most important Theory Y principle.)

Just do it!

You can't develop a winning management style simply by reading this guide or a dozen other books. You develop a style and incorporate its elements into your patterned behavioral responses by trying them out and seeing which ones work. Once you are sure that the tools and behaviors mentioned here work, *just do it.*

Just do it! Like riding a bicycle or trying roller blades for the first time, there is some uncertainty. Suppose you fall?

Suppose you fail? Suppose you succeed? You won't know until you try.

People with Winning Management Styles

Throughout this guide, we've provided some sample text to give you an idea of what to say to employees, but these won't be the words you'll use. Find the words and phrases that work for you and the people with whom you're interacting. Your discussions and messages have to be and look and sound natural and sincere.

A winning management style is, after all, a very personal thing—it looks different on different people. It is based on the same beliefs and attitudes about people, however. Here are some thumbnail sketches of people I've met who each have a distinctive and winning management style:

- A former middle school principal-turned-HR manager, smooth and almost too cool, but very effective in a young company.

- A retired U.S.A.F. master sergeant, an in-your-face, profane man who insists on participation and high-levels of performance—and gets it.

- A petite woman who carries around a clipboard for notes and task lists and doesn't take no for an answer. (*"WHO SAYS you can't fire people in the federal government?"*)

- A quiet, white-haired Irishman, literally with twinkling eyes, who sits on the sidelines and chuckles with amusement—but he gets things done.

- A stoop-shouldered, confrontational, abrupt man who's always fuming about managerial oversights, but who is a proven profit maker.

- A woman with flaming red hair and a temperament to match, who shocks people into delivering higher levels of performance.

- A retired Marine Corps gunnery sergeant who delights in beating the system—and gets extraordinary performance from his people.

These are actual people. If you put them together in the same room, they might not be able to function effectively as a group, but each has built strong relationships with co-workers and direct reports, developed people others have ignored, and taken ordinary or failing groups and turned them into outstanding teams.

Whatever your personal style, it likely will fit somewhere within the styles represented by this group of people. Just incorporate the attitudes and beliefs we've been talking about, and go for it. Your own unique winning management style will come through.

Along the way, you will make a positive difference in the lives of those with whom you work, and a lot of money for the company that employs you.

Chapter 10

Your Communication Style

W e've provided examples of what a winning management style looks like, but this is just the beginning of
the process. The centerpiece of a top designer's new collection really won't take shape until a model puts it on and
strides down the runway in her own individual way, allowing
the garment to express itself (this is why supermodels earn so
much).

One of the challenges to helping people become great
managers is that the values needed to support and sustain a
true Theory Y management style are not yet there, or are present only nominally. It's one thing to read or talk about
allowing people to participate in making the decisions that
affect them, and quite another to sit at the head of the table
and say, "What do you guys think we ought to do?" At that
point, you're committed to accept what you hear and to discuss the options they come up with.

The value of the input you receive will depend on
whether or not others around the table believe you want their
input. You have to believe in them and demonstrate this faith
in a variety of ways before they will believe in you and share
their thoughts and suggestions.

For example, most people socialized in the West are
familiar with the basic tenets of "fairness." Still, many will
take unfair advantage of others if it is entertaining or
profitable. Almost everyone cheats just a little bit, and
virtually every employee has felt at one time or another that
he or she has been cheated by a manager.

> What have *you* done to establish yourself as a manager who treats employees fairly?

Everyone believes he or she is as fair as most people, but that is not what makes us ethical, honest, or trustworthy in the minds of those who watch our behavior the way direct reports watch their manager. Therefore, before creating any expectations in anyone's mind about participation, you need to establish yourself as someone who delivers on commitments.

When Parry studied the research data he collected from managers, he concluded that it was not enough to say that someone was "Theory X" or "Theory Y" in their practice of management. Neither was it sufficient to think that someone could "put on" a management style like a cloak when arriving at the office or plant.

Indeed, something more was needed to make these classifications more precise. Parry decided to identify values that were common among successful managers and values that individuals could strengthen in order to improve their performance as managers.

Many values were identified, fairness among them. But to get the many down to a manageable level, Parry and his researchers organized the values into eight categories or descriptors that combine strengths, attitudes, and preferences. Four represent *personal* style, and four represent *communication* style. The program he developed includes a methodology for measuring commitment to each of the eight values, as well as a means by which an individual can strengthen specific values.

(Reading this book is no substitute for taking part in a managerial assessment program. However, it can provide some helpful concepts that will significantly enhance your experience as a participant in the program.)

In this chapter, we present Parry's eight values or style components, along with descriptive information and examples so you can identify your own value-orientation.

Understanding Your Personal Style

- Are you a *thinker,* hungry for details?
- Are you an *intuitor,* looking for the big picture?
- Are you a *sensor,* pulling information out of the environment?
- Are you a *feeler,* working from your gut instincts?

The ways of behaving that constitute a style are referred to by some as "personality traits." However, I prefer to think of them in terms of habits and routines—ways of organizing and sharing information. Habits, routines, and "ways" are subject to change if the individual sees a need to do so and disciplines himself to do a few specific things differently until he becomes more comfortable with the change effort. That just seems to make more sense. Besides, it reduces the possibility that individuals will decide that they are "stuck" and just can't change. Really, anyone can change if there are payoffs along the way and at the end of the effort. The suggestions offered in this book will lead to payoffs!

Empathy and Communication Style:
Being Accessible to Others

Parry identified four descriptors for personal communication style: *empathic, critical, searching,* and *advising.* These four ways of interacting with others are the major determinants of your communication style; they either tend to draw others in, or push them away.

Understanding Your Communication Style

- Are you *empathic,* tuning in to others' concerns?
- Are you able to make *critical* distinctions?
- Are you good at *searching* and digging out solution data?
- Are you good at *advising,* coaching, and counseling?

Each of these four descriptors lies on a negative–positive continuum: unattractive behavior on one end, and behavior that attracts others on the other end. As an illustration, consider this pair of opposites for being empathetic:

"Why are you telling me this stuff?"
vs.
"I can really feel your pain!"

Which approach is likely to attract others and encourage them to come to you? Which will create warm and welcome feelings in the minds of people who report to you? And which will cause people to withdraw or withhold their feelings?

Do you care? Do you want to be an approachable manager? Or do you want people to keep you at a respectful distance? A manager can do and be all the Theory Y things described above, yet still be considered cold. If you think your effectiveness is limited because people think of you as cold, unfeeling, or unsympathetic, maybe you can make a greater effort to tune in to people who are trying to share personal information with you (*My mother died; my dog got run over by a delivery truck; the transmission fell out of my car; my best friend's boyfriend shot her last night*).

Why *do* you want to know about people's lives? Maybe you don't, but social convention and practical experience say that the whole person comes to work. So deal with the whole person! Sometimes that means allowing them to share the things that are foremost in their minds, so they can focus on the work they have to do.

> The whole person comes to work, so you'll have to deal with the whole person.

Is there a Theory Y way to do this? Of course. Many of them. But the idea is to give people 30 seconds of undivided attention, and then break the connection. Say something soothing, such as "I know that must have been distressing to you." Then say something like, "If you'll excuse me, I have to make a call. But do let me know later today how you're doing with the combined project report." That closing remark returns the relationship to business.

Is there a Theory X way to deal with kind of situation? Of course. All you have to do is assume that the other person, like you, has a childish need to share his or her latest excitement. If you're going to get any work out of this person, you need to sit for several minutes and listen.

But be warned: There are a lot of people who want to tug at their manager's heartstrings to escape close scrutiny of poor performance. In one such episode, a weak performer told his manager, "You know, I was a premature baby."

The manager, astounded, said, "You have a premature baby?"

"No," he replied, almost proudly. "I was one!" Not about to get sucked into that "poor me" game, the manager said, "What does that have to do with your failure to do the work you've been assigned? What we need to talk about is your performance today and from now on. As far as I'm concerned, that's the *only* important issue."

That's a pure Theory Y response, a call for adult behavior and problem solving. Not really harsh, but certainly direct.

How much empathy do you want to convey? How much more is needed? This is a place where specific feedback would be particularly helpful, either from someone who feels short-changed by you or someone who has observed transactions that did not have satisfactory conclusions. With that kind of feedback and a little discussion about what more you should do or say, your ability to respond empathetically can be increased.

Is there an employee who feels secure enough to give you that kind of feedback? Or that you trust enough to ask?

The ability to respond empathetically is just one of the four legs of the communication platform. By the time the other three are reviewed, you should have a better feel for what "communication style" means.

Critical Ability and Communication Style

The ability to be *critical* is kind of a mixed blessing. People say, "He's so *critical*. I can't do anything right!" And yet, what is the purpose of a manager, if not to judge and determine what's okay and what's not up to standard, and then to give people that information?

In terms of management style, critical ability is a strong component of Theory X: the wise parent instructing the child. Some people are comfortable with this, on both the giving and the receiving end of the transaction, but most people aren't.

Somewhere out there is the idea of "unconditional love" that is supposed to exist between parents, children, and soulmates. It calls for suspension of judgment—accepting others where and how they are at any given moment, without holding back appreciation or support (even if there is provocation or disappointment). It is certainly an ideal to consider. In the real world, some things are *not* okay. Some work *doesn't* meet standards. And *someone* has to be the defender of predetermined criteria of okay-ness.

It is important for organizations to make sure each individual understands the standards and regulations related to the work they do, and the criteria that will be used to assess the quality of that work.

Consider these managerial responses to an imperfect situation:

"That's the dumbest thing you've done yet!"

vs.

"I'm surprised you would find that an adequate response."

Both responses confront the fact that something non-standard has been done. One of them slams the door to constructive conversation and condemns the relationship to some kind of purgatory until either the employee or the manager leaves. The other response is just as firm in expressing the manager's disapproval, but it opens the door to dialogue and to the possibility of going forward constructively to maintain and even improve an existing working relationship.

To be effective at building strong relationships with the people on your team and improving the quality of work performed, you have to be able to criticize work without criticizing the individual—to say that the work is not okay without also sending the message that the person is not okay, either.

A winning management style conveys non-conforming performance information, but leaves the door open to having a continuing problem-solving relationship. Everyone makes imperfect decisions from time to time, and everyone occasionally disappoints a friend or manager. Life happens.

So, when it comes to basic communication, we can narrow down our responses to just two kinds: those that damage relationships, and those that leave the door open for constructive outcomes in the future. (Sometimes, slamming a door is not a bad idea. Just think before you act.)

> There are two kinds of responses: those that damage relationships, and those that leave the door open for future relationships.

When a worker's performance disappoints, the manager often takes it as a personal affront or a test of the relationship. (*He knows better than that! Why would he do something so stupid?*)

This is where the boundary between *I/thou* and *me/you* needs to be scrupulously observed. Whatever the reason or the circumstance, people choose. They choose to conform or perform, or they choose to do something else. Unless you are a Theory X "parent" down to your bones, you have to accept that some choices made by adults have nothing to do with you.

> Adults have the freedom to choose, but they also have a responsibility to accept the consequences of those decisions.

Manager, be clear about the limits of your responsibilities.

A television preacher some years ago expressed such a dispassionate assessment this way: "If you're considering suicide, just don't leave a mess for someone else to clean up."

Searching and Communication Style

Searching is perhaps the ultimate in adult-adult relationships. It happens when two or more adults work together to find workable, mutually satisfying solutions. Gordon Lippitt spoke eloquently about this searching process some years ago. Lippitt developed a compellingly simple problem-solving model with only three elements:

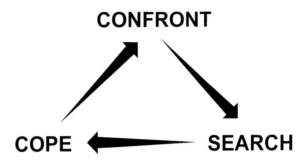

CONFRONT

COPE ← **SEARCH**

The model was developed to solve various social problems associated with the Civil Rights movement, but its very simplicity makes it widely applicable wherever adult-adult relationships are operating. The starting point, according to Lippitt, is to *confront* the fact that there is a problem. There is no problem-solving unless those involved will admit that there is a problem. [1]

Once a problem is acknowledged, the group can begin the *search* process by looking for a workable but usually interim solution. ("Okay, let's try this for a couple of months and see what happens.")

Next, the group negotiates ways to *cope* with the imperfection of the interim solution (there might be a schedule of follow-up meetings to discuss progress or problems). But the most powerful coping mechanism is the ability to *confront* the fact that things are not working as planned (materials are still late), that people are not behaving as promised ("Dave" is still abusing sick leave), or that the system still is not performing satisfactorily (payments to vendors are not being issued on time).

Lippitt glossed over a couple of steps in creating his model, but I've shared it with thousands of managers, and no one has failed to understand its elements or failed to understand the first step:

Confront things and people when performance is in conflict with expectations.

This is a major lesson for managers. The verb *confront* has a negative connotation, perhaps because we witness so much ugly confrontation on TV. But the truth is that where performance is concerned, there is no progress without confronting the facts about costs, profits, and return on investment (ROI). And about targets, and missing them by *how much?*

More truth: Many managers working in our litigious society are afraid to address poor performance if minorities are involved. Employees who do meet performance standards become demoralized and cannot help but lose some respect for their manager and other leaders when they see slackers and underperformers getting away with it. More than anything else, this makes the argument that managers must search for ways to measure performance and contributions that are so clear and unambiguous that they are virtually free of race or sex differentiation.

Maintaining the "searching" process will be challenging, but it is an essential management task. That's what continuous performance improvement is all about—the quest for better, faster, cheaper solutions.

The Theory Y motive behind this quest is rooted in the manager's ability and desire to communicate, to pull other workers into the search process by involving them in meaningful use of their intelligence and experience. That means including them in the quest for excellence and for better, faster, cheaper ways to work, for improved ROI, and for ways for all to obtain greater satisfaction from the work they do and the relationships involved.

This is where the hot-cold dichotomy fits in: How involved and invested are people in ongoing searching or development processes? Are there systematic efforts being made to address continuing problems/glitches in the work flow? Are individuals being rewarded for their contributions? This is another source of motive power.

These kinds of questions can help you clarify some of the neglected dimensions of the manager's job. A winning management style is the result of a lot of thinking and experimenting, and a lot of personal growth.

Advising Others

Advising is a function with many faces. In Theory X management, the "wise parent" is counseling the "inexperienced" child. But there are many other ways that advising can be used to build relationships and to communicate encouragement and support.

Most managers have access to information that employees don't have access to, and most possess more experience in the organization and knowledge of opportunities within it. The manager can choose to use that information to benefit employees, or assume that no one will be interested in it. If no one expresses a desire to achieve or advance, the manager might stop looking for opportunities to pass along.

Advising does not have to be a solemn, formal process (as in the old master and the naïve pupil). More likely, it will be a brief exchange at the water cooler or in the hallway. "Gene, have you ever considered...?" or maybe "Sally, while you're home on maternity leave, would you be interested in doing some telecommuting?" In both instances, the manager can say, "If that interests you, stop by my office this afternoon and let's talk."

The manager has planted an idea. If it takes root, the employee will show up in the afternoon. If not, then at least the offer was made. On to someone and something else.

We mentioned mentoring earlier. It can be extremely rewarding for all concerned, but the manager should look for someone with the right mix of ability, desire, and discipline. Unfortunately, those three things don't always appear at the same time in the same person. Communication is important for both people in any mentoring relationship.

Mentoring

Here is a simplified description of the mentoring process. You've no doubt had some experience with it and have seen the power of this unique form of managerial communication.

Steps in the mentoring process are:

1. Input from mentor
2. Application
3. Results
4. Debriefing
5. Planning the next steps

And always feedback, ASAP.

The mentoring process can go on for months, and even years. Sometimes it takes only a short period of time to get someone launched, but this happens only when advising is really up-close and personal—when the mentor shares his or her experience and passes along advice about things to do, but also introduces the mentee to others who can help them. Blessed are those who provide this kind of professional nurturing, this special kind of communication. Fortunate are those who receive it.

Summing It All Up

As you can see, a communication style is more than tone of voice—it's the music. Put that together with Theory Y behavior and you have a winning combination.

At this point, you should have a good idea about how to improve your communication style. Try to enlist a partner in your personal improvement process. To improve, we need targets (things we want to do differently), but we also need someone to assess the effect of our efforts. Feedback is the key. Fast feedback, continuous feedback, and small celebrations when you get it right.

In every interaction, it's important to signal to new colleagues or long-time associates, "I'm open to connecting with you, working with you, contributing to your success."

Remember, the essence of effective communication is not only to get people to do what you want them to do, but also to build trust and rapport and make them part of *your* team. When your words and music are coordinated, your winning management style takes shape.

The manager's message is connecting at the *feeling* level, and that's where the "dance" with others begins. Or sometimes ends. A true story:

Florence was a beautiful young woman with auburn hair, blue eyes, and a statuesque figure. She also had an MBA and was regional sales manager for a leading pharmaceutical firm. Florence was dating an equally attractive man who was an executive with (and heir to) a sporting goods company. It looked like a perfect match, but suddenly, inexplicably, it was off. Florence's sister provided the answer. "Tom was too tentative about everything. Maybe he was just trying to please her, but the message she got was that he might turn out to be weak and ineffectual, and she just couldn't handle that."

Somewhere in that dance, Tom miscommunicated. Or perhaps he didn't. Maybe Florence read him like a book, and took flight.

Lovers are not the only people who look for certainty, self-assurance, and confidence. People at work are no less discerning in their readings of one another, and in particular, of their managers. There is what is called a "feeling-tone" in every communication, and effective managers learn how to use their messages to convey information at several levels of communication. One level is content, of course. Another is tone (*I'm pleased with your performance; I'm displeased with your behavior; I like you; I find it hard to be near you*). Tone communicates!

87

But there is another component to a winning management style, and it is your *personal style.* We'll look at that next.

Chapter 10 Note

1. Gordon Lippitt was a professor at George Washington University. He introduced this model at the annual Conference of Friends (Quakers) in Philadelphia in 1966.

Chapter 11

Your Personal Style

W ho are you, really? How do you think? How do you make decisions? What are you trying to accomplish? Almost everyone has been asked these kinds of questions.

They have to do with *feelings, sensing, intuition,* and *thinking*—the four components of what Perry's Managerial Assessment of Proficiency refers to as *personal style*. They are important components of a winning management style.

Feelings and Personal Style

What do feelings have to do with one's personal style? Maybe everything. We talked earlier about beliefs and values. It is in the *feelings* domain that beliefs and values reside and operate.

Would a manager with deeply held convictions about planning and organizing make the same decisions as a manager committed to building strong teams and personal bonding among team members? Do deeply held beliefs and values direct an individual to know the right things to do, and do they give him or her the courage to do them?

Let me relate a true story from my own experience. Seven 17-man teams at an oil refinery were undergoing a performance analysis. Everyone involved thought the Red Jackets would win. The team got its name because their manager, a former Marine, got all 17 team members to wear matching red jackets. He organized numerous social events for team members and their wives, and couples participated in a bowling league. They even shared ownership in a ski boat and associated equipment. The Red Jackets were a really tight, well-organized team—or so everyone thought. Actually, the team came in sixth out of seven when the performance analysis was complete. The winning team was managed by a quiet man who never socialized with his team after work. As a matter of fact, the team members themselves did not appear to socialize with each other. Who would have guessed?

What made the difference? The leader of the winning team believed in thinking ahead, planning, and organizing. He organized the next day's work before leaving the refinery each night, collecting the tools, equipment, and any special materials his team would need and pre-staging them for his team to pick up the next morning.

Within minutes after the 8:00 a.m. starting time, his team members were all at work, while members of the other teams were still wandering around the equipment shed, getting organized for the day. (An estimated one week of worker time was "lost" every morning between 8:00 a.m. and 9:00 a.m. in the equipment shed.)

I tell you this true story to make a couple of important points:

Strong team spirit and effective performance do not correlate positively in all instances.

Good feelings about one's team and co-workers are nice, but they are not critical for noteworthy performance.

Good feelings do not substitute for more tangible processes, such as planning, organizing, and pre-staging materials.

Feelings can be used to mask inadequate performance.

Feelings, values, and beliefs are powerful determinants of activity. For example, what do you care about? Being recognized? Being effective? Being popular with your co-workers? And what do your co-workers care about? Loose standards? Casual time–discipline? Personal advancement? Parties? Quitting early on Fridays?

Unavoidably, beliefs and values will be reflected in every decision a manager makes. What "feels" right? The high road of discipline, or something looser and less authoritarian?

There is some "go along and get along" in most managerial decision making.

Questions and issues like these positioned Theory Y management as an ideal. The Theory Y manager, in theory at least, will always take the high road, strive for the greater good, and eventually persuade co-workers to join in the effort (or leave for another job). On the hot-cold, high-low scale, what things do *you* feel strongly about? What things might you feel more strongly about? What things *should* you feel more strongly about if you are to achieve higher productivity?

As always, start by making a list. Maybe a 15-minute exercise in a staff meeting could create some understanding of what kinds of values matter to the group. That might be a good place to begin the process of changing relationships within the group and between the group and the rest of the organization. Ask your team members to list the five values that drive the team. Once the responses are shared, go into a second exercise by giving this instruction. Ask them to individually rank their values on a scale of 1–5: #1 is the most important, and #5 is the least important.

A third exercise, and one that could continue, might be a discussion based on the question "What have we done this week to reflect the values we say we believe in?"

Thinking and Personal Style

Opposite the soft logic of feelings is the hard logic of *thinking*—making decisions on the basis of research and documented experiences that can be replicated as the basis of decision making. Like F. W. Taylor measuring shovelfuls of coal. Like all the long-ago guys in white lab coats who walked around industrial workplaces with stopwatches and clipboards, doing time-and-motion studies.

A manager who once operated a lathe in a large plant once worked with "a nice kid" who was a member of the stopwatch brigade. "We all liked him and wanted him to succeed. When we saw him coming, we would do things like push the stock bench away so we would have to take several steps to pick up stock to mount on the lathe. Then he could say something like, 'Bob, wouldn't it be easier if you rolled the stock bench closer?' And I could say, 'What a great idea! Why didn't I think of that?'"

Thinking, of course, is important. Remembering and incorporating recent data is essential in project management, but a kind of operational paralysis can set in when you get stuck in the cognitive process. This happens sometimes when we think alone, ignoring competent co-workers who are standing by, ready to help. This kind of excessive thinking is truly an example of Theory X at work. Ego, pride, or even fear of "group think" keeps people from using such powerful techniques as brainstorming, mind-mapping, and other exercises that can bring collective brainpower to bear on a problem. Avoid isolating yourself. It will limit your options and keep you from examining all the issues.

The need to win and be right drives people to ignore obvious clues and revert to destructive competitive behavior. The power experience of thinking together (collaborative decision making) is one of the benefits of formal training, but the imperative to compete and win is so strong in the culture of many organizations that managers forget about the rich resources sitting around the table.

The managers of a company that had recently been convicted of price fixing learned this lesson at one of their retreats. A group exercise was in progress, and ten teams of eight managers each were locked into noisy, win-lose competition. The senior manager in charge had finally had enough of the cutthroat behavior. He jumped on top of a table and started shouting:

"Don't you people read the papers? Don't you know what has happened to our company? Don't you have the decency to feel the disgrace that colors us all? Can't you see yourselves now, doing the same kinds of dishonest and unethical things that are the shame of this company? Can't you think past your need for one-upmanship, to win at someone else's expense? Can't you see the mind trap you've fallen into?

"And don't try to blame the consultants. I heard the same instructions you did. They never told you to cheat or to lie in negotiations. You brought that behavior with you into this room.

"Look at yourselves! Look at the people you're trying to cheat. Will they ever trust you again? What happens when we get back to work next week? Do you think they will forget your behavior on this day? How can we save and re-build a company full of people as unethical as you have proved yourselves to be today?

"Pay attention to this lesson, and don't ever let me catch any of you thinking that cheating is the way to win, or that lying is the way to get ahead. If I do, I promise I will fire you on the spot!"

The teachable moment had arrived. A lesson had been pounded home to 80 managers, good men and true, who were loyal to their points of view and to their ways of thinking. They had reverted to thought processes that were grooved into their brains like the winter ruts in a back-country dirt road. Despite all the recent news coverage and loss of the value of stock they all owned, they had not even considered behaving or thinking differently, and it never occurred to them that much of what was in their heads might actually be wrong for the times.

This is why *thinking* is one of the four elements of personal style that are considered necessary for managerial proficiency. Processing information and accessing it for decision making is one of the things managers are paid to do. The larger challenge is for managers to continue asking themselves something like, *Am I trying to solve today's problem on the basis of yesterday's solution?*

Sensing and Personal Style

The next important element in a manager's personal style is *sensing*. The manager as sensor pulls input from the environment, reading and feeling the vibes. Sensing is about *acquiring data.*

Have you ever walked into your house and instantly had the feeling that someone else had been there, for good or evil? Have you ever been with friends and had a gut feeling that their relationship is on the rocks? Or walked into a conference room and sensed that something ugly was about to happen (such as someone getting fired or being accused of theft)?

Sensing or reading "signs" in the environment, like a tracker in the wild, is a good way to obtain information that can usually be confirmed. Being able to "sense" an opportunity and to respond to it is a powerful advantage for a manager.

We operate in a sea of information, but most of us don't tune in because we are either preoccupied with some immediate personal issue or hampered by character flaws (self-centeredness, indifference, insensitivity to others, etc.). The manager can be a member of Mensa, but if he or she is oblivious to the needs of others, who will want to help him succeed?

A true story: After several hours leading a seminar with local managers of an international delivery firm, the consultant spoke privately with the senior manager. "I don't know what it is, but that guy Tom is dirty. He's doing something behind the scenes that's dishonest and probably illegal." Startled by the consultant's comment, the manager revealed that Tom was secretly being investigated by corporate security, the local police, and Interpol.

What did the consultant pick up on, in a roomful of strangers? What was there about Tom that attracted the consultant's attention and led to the gut feeling that Tom was "dirty"? The consultant couldn't explain anything in detail. "I was watching him, and suddenly I just *knew!*"

In another real situation, an HR manager stopped on the way to a meeting to observe his company's drilling crew in an unguarded moment. He noticed a lot of reckless behavior, and had a feeling that a disaster was on the horizon. He wrote the president a memo, advising him to consider selling the drilling operation and outsourcing that function. "One serious accident can pull all the profit out of that operation for the next several years," he explained in the memo. The memo was forwarded to the drilling manager, and the HR manager was subjected to a lot of verbal abuse.

But two weeks later, a member of the drilling crew was hospitalized after he was nearly cut in half by a cable. Within the following month, the drilling operation was sold.

What information was the manager acting on? And why did he decide to stick his neck out and say something?

The answer to the first question has to do with being aware of second- and third-order consequences—things that will happen as a result of a current situation. As to why he said something, when we sense impending disaster, don't we have a moral imperative to report it? Or are people afraid to act on such visions, afraid to be subjected to ridicule when asked, "So where did you get your information?"

Intuition and Personal Style

Intuition is not the sole prerogative of women. A man is more likely to say, "I had a hunch" or "You can't beat that old gut feel," but it's still intuition. That "gut feel" is really a mish-mash of old experiences and ideas that merge around a present problem. It gets sorted out in a way that lets the manager say something like, "No, not that. Here's what we're going to do!" An amazing plan pops onto the scene, seemingly out of nowhere.

One consultant described the feeling this way: "Usually, I know within 15 minutes where the gold is buried, but it takes a couple of days of spooking around to be able to defend what I knew from the start."

In group meetings where things are stalled, someone gets a feeling that "Frank" will have the answer. Frank is asked what he thinks, and he really does know.

We've all had these experiences, but we don't all trust them. *Intuition* is one of a manager's "success secrets," closely linked with sensing: sensing is about acquiring data. Intuition is about using data.

One More Element of Personal Style

Moral courage has to be included as a component of a winning management style, even though it's not part of the MAP proficiency assessment. What's the purpose of all these competencies if one does not possess the confidence to act? A manager should be confident enough to say "No! This will not happen on my watch," or "Someone who can make the decision needs to know. *Now!*"

In these politically correct and litigious times, there are a lot of impediments to garden-variety courage and truth-telling. That's an unfortunate reality. Some managers with families and mortgages think they cannot afford to be stand-up people who speak up on behalf of others.

But this is one of the real tests of a manager's style: Will my manager back me up if something goes wrong or blows up or money is lost or a client withdraws a contract? Or will he or she just shrug and say, "Well, I tried to warn you..."

Why should anyone work unpaid overtime, come early, stay late, and make every effort to support a manager who will not reciprocate in the unlikely event a subordinate's job is on the line? They won't—at least not by choice.

Why should hourly workers, maybe working for minimum wage, exert extra effort for a manager who won't fight for the small salary increases available to them or who won't spring for the occasional case of soda, or a manager who is anal or legalistic about adhering to work "rules" when someone has a sick kid at home?

Every worker deserves a manager who has the personal and communicative competencies we've been talking about—someone who also believes that people ought to have a voice in determining how they are used at work. But more than that, real people at work want action. They want a voice speaking on their behalf. They want someone who believes in them and wants them to be treated fairly more than they want personal recognition and a promotion. Is that too much to ask?

> What's the purpose of being competent as a manager if you lack confidence and moral courage?

The flat organizational model is gradually becoming universal, but chain-of-command logic is still at work in most organizations. Managers still are expected to align themselves with senior management, even if it means going against the people they supervise. Who wants to bite the hand that feeds them?

A last thought on this track: Many managers were never workers, and certainly never workers-for-life. How well do they understand the people they supervise—their motives and concerns, and their view of the organization from the bottom up? Sometimes, even well-intentioned managers misunderstand or misinterpret what they see and hear among non-supervisory staff.

Chapter 12

Coming to Grips with Management Style

Once an individual is appointed manager or team leader, the work group has a boss. Employees will exhibit a certain amount of compliance, regardless of who the boss is, and that is probably where many if not most work groups are on any given day: minimally compliant. As the old saying goes, *"The boss ain't always right, but he is always the boss!"*

Management becomes more interesting to leaders who think of it as a *non-authoritarian* way to get more than the minimum out of workers, or to improve ROI on payroll without having a union. For some managers, the elements of a winning management style we've talked about are easy, natural, and already a part of their way of being and thinking. If these behaviors aren't natural, however, they can be learned.

It's sometimes helpful to socialize with employees over and above mandatory company functions, but it's not usually necessary. In fact, the old prohibitions regarding fraternizing are not without merit. It's harder to remain objective when the manager identifies too closely with certain members of the group or develops social friendships with some people and not others. It can also create tension within the team. However, there are exceptions to every rule, and some managers can manage both kinds of relationships with few consequences. Others cannot.

The role of manager can be filled by any number of people, most of whom would get essentially the same results. The appointment is generally conditional on performance and results, and it is the workers, to a surprising extent, who are in control here.

It follows, then, that if the managers and the workers are working together without unresolved conflicts, more work will get done. Maybe work will get done *better, faster,* and *cheaper,* guaranteeing success for the manager and job security for all (assuming that corporate-level plans haven't already been made to downsize, outsource, or restructure). Management is the manipulation of variables, some of which are people. No one likes to be manipulated, and workers are very quick to pick up on superficial concern and empty promises. If the manager can engage employees in becoming partners in the enterprise and give them some strings to pull on their own, their behavior and orientation toward the company will change. They will *choose* to behave differently. Is that then a manipulation? Or does it matter?

Once non-supervisory employees are given strings to pull and decisions to make that are independent of their manager, other strengths and capabilities will most likely emerge that the manager can vector into still more productivity and job satisfaction for the workers. Fewer people will call in sick, and morale no doubt will improve as well (when morale is good, there is less clutter and less messiness in work areas, and workers' personal appearance will improve).

At some point down this developmental path, many of the manager's most tedious chores will have been assumed by others. He or she will be free to do more coaching, counseling, planning, and looking good to senior management! The speed of this journey will depend on how readily workers accept the manager and how wounded they have been by other managers. It will also depend on the extent to which they see the manager as honest in his or her efforts to boost workers and to reward them for *their* efforts.

The elements and competencies of a winning managerial style I am presenting here have already helped thousands of managers to succeed in some of the best companies in the United States. Don't diminish the importance of any of them. Intuition and sensitivity might, for example, seem airy-fairy to some people, but in a lot of organizations, they constitute the difference between making $8 an hour or $200 a day. So, pay attention and try not to judge any of these suggestions as silly until you have tried them yourself.

A Crazy Idea?

Consider this scenario: A new manager has been brought in to take over a group that's worked together for several years under a succession of managers. Maybe the new manager is younger than some of the group's members. Maybe he or she is from a minority ethnic group (in which case some workers will probably conclude that they got a "quota" manager).

As usual, there are no secrets; anyone with eyes and ears knows what's going on in the company. The new manager, at the first staff meeting, asks the work group something like this:

> "What do you expect from me? I've heard you weren't too happy with your last manager, and that maybe he didn't last in this job because you didn't let him. I want to last in this job, and I know that this won't happen unless we work together.

"So, tell me what you want and what you expect, and I'll do my best to make things work out for all of us. I'm ready to consider anything you say, and I will give us time to discuss what I hear you saying."

What do you think of that? The tone of voice and his facial expressions will be good clues to his management style. Suppose the workers sit in shock and disbelief, unable to say a thing? If that happens, the manager can say something like, "If any of you decide to give me the benefit of your suggestions, I'll be easy to find." He then adjourns the meeting, and it's back to business.

To be sure, members of the group will talk a lot among themselves, and perhaps they will acknowledge that they owe the new manager their support. Probably, the discussion of what they want from the new manager will never take place. Maybe they have already received what they wanted.

The point I'm trying to make is that what a new manager should do is call on the existing work group to start over by creating adult-adult relationships, instead of playing the old game in which the boss was a frustrated parent and workers were petulant children.

It's as Simple as You Want to Make It

A managerial proficiency assessment will present you with clear choices: Adopt the Theory X style and assume a traditional, top-down way of managing, or adopt a Theory Y style and confront the need to reconsider a lot of what you believe or think you believe.

Theory X management can be respectable and respectful, but it doesn't put much of a premium on personal growth and development. Neither does it require much in the way of managerial self-analysis, unless you have trouble meeting your numbers.

Theory Y, by contrast, is full of challenge and opportunity, and it is the way into the future. With Theory Y, employees are trusted to do all the right things right and assume responsibilities on their own—responsibilities imagined by Theory X managers.

Other Paths to Theory Y

Open-book management is an exciting new kind of management. The term refers to the simple premise that employees have a right to contribute to the success of their company. The company's books are "open" so employees can see what money comes in and how it's spent and can participate in setting production and financial targets. Usually, there's an opportunity for employees to participate in stock ownership and bonus programs that reinforce their commitment to the company's success.

When workers know that their daily activities and choices will make an impact on the company's bottom line and on their share of the profit, many of the usual management challenges such as motivating people and asking for their ideas become totally unnecessary.

Open-book management was the creation of Jack Stack, president of Springfield Remanufacturing (an auto and truck engine rebuilding company). Stack wrote a great book about the experience of purchasing the company on an Employee

Stock Ownership Plan, which he titled *The Great Game of Business.*[1] In it, Stack asked one of the most important questions ever posed to the business community: "How can you expect workers to help companies make money when workers don't know how companies make money?" Stack developed a 40-hour course on business economics, and required all his employees to attend. After the course, every employee could read and understand an annual report and develop a business plan. The program provided such extraordinary results that Stack had to form a separate profit center to handle all the demands from other companies for plant visits and for representatives to participate in the game.

You would think a great new idea like this would catch everyone's attention, but it hasn't. At least one company trying to move in the direction of open book management allocated a fixed 40% of total revenues for salaries; the only way people can earn more in such companies is to increase the size of that 40% pool (which means increasing profits or reducing expenses). But is that incentive enough to break their habits of internal competition, where divisions tend to withhold even customer information from other parts of the organization? It will take a change in attitude and organizational culture that incorporates the principles of Theory Y, but I believe it is worth the work.

Another approach to incorporating Theory Y values was based on the writings of psychiatrist M. Scott Peck, most famous for writing *The Road Less Traveled* in 1978. It was his 1987 book *The Different Drum: Community Making and Peace* that supported the idea that community-building works as well in for-profit companies as it does in organizing community groups. Peck and some of his followers organized themselves in 1984 as the Foundation for Community Enlightenment, logging extraordinary results with all the usual corporate criteria (such as profit, performance, growth, reduced turnover) by following Peck's prescriptions for authentic relationships.[2] The Foundation for Community Enlightenment was disbanded in 2002. Its activities are continued through a network called Community Crossroads.[3]

Another thread of Theory Y advocacy emerged 15 years after McGregor introduced Theory Y. Abraham Maslow (famous for Maslow's Hierarchy of Needs) wrote a book titled *Eupsychian Management*, which translates as "good mental health management." In the 1965 work, Maslow spelled out all the values usually associated with Theory Y in 36 propositions (open-book management's tenets are reflective of Maslow's values). What made this book unusual is that it was based on observations made by Maslow in his first experience in a corporate setting. He was invited to be a scholar-in-residence at Non-Linear Systems in California for the summer of 1962; *Eupsychian Management* was a result of that experience. It's worth tracking down.[4]

There are many other researchers and management-model builders who are not mentioned here. But for a short introduction to creating a winning management style, the framework suggested in the work of McGregor, Maslow, Peck, Parry, and Stack should provide an adequate structure for you to begin formulating your own.

Read! Study! If management is your chosen profession, you need to honor that decision with continuous input from which you can refine and reinforce the elements of your management style. There will always be more things to learn, more skills to strengthen, and new strategies to try.

Don't be intellectually lazy—don't cheat yourself.

Chapter 12 Notes

1. Jack Stack's *The Great Game of Business* might be one of the most influential management books since McGregor's *The Human Side of Enterprise*. See www.greatgame.com.

2. Dr. Peck wrote 15 books. The organization intervention methodology he advocated involved four stages: pseudocommunity, chaos, emptiness, and community. He died in 2005.

3. http://communityx-roads.org

4. Maslow's journal notes from his observations at Non-Linear Systems in California became *Eupsychian Management*. In it, he extended the Theory Y thinking of McGregor and anticipated the quality movement, as well as extended his own ideas about self-actualization.

Chapter 13

Wrapping Up

Creating a winning management style has to become your own personal development project. No one has it all, but all of us have bits and pieces *and* the opportunity to build on our strengths and compensate for our weaknesses. The process will be fun!

Going to work is a necessity for most people, but that doesn't mean it has to be drudgery. Managers with the opportunity to build careers for themselves and others can take an "ordinary" group of people and turn them into a winning production team. What could be more fun that that?

And think of the celebrations! It's almost a crime for a group of people to meet a challenging deadline and not have some kind of celebration. Shame on the manager who allows that to happen.

Finding a Safe Place to Try on New Behaviors

Time. Patience. Testing. These three elements should be considered by anyone who wants to develop a new, more-effective management style.

First, it takes *time* to determine what you want to do differently, and you will have to admit to yourself that some of your interpersonal skills are deficient (which is difficult for some people to admit). You'll also need to set some specific targets and arrange with someone to provide feedback on your progress. This can be painful (and funny).

Second, it will take *patience* on the part of the people you live with. Watch out the first time you say to your spouse/ friend, *"I know you're upset. Could you tell me what's bothering you?"* The other person will either get angrier, or make you angry by laughing at you. And you probably should avoid telling a teenager, *"I know what's bothering you, and I feel your pain."*

Some testing is necessary, but probably only a limited bit at home. Why not get involved with a church group or take an evening class, or join a hobby group? Most communities badly need volunteers to get involved in all sorts of civic, professional, and neighborhood groups. Find places where you are not well known, so you can try out new behaviors without being obvious. See how strangers or acquaintances react; the feedback (reactions) you get will more likely reflect your impact on them, rather than their expectations of you.

Authoritarian Theory X behavior doesn't play well in most adult volunteer organizations. With apologies for a personal reference, one of my best learning experiences came when I was required to spend a semester working with an organization different from my paid work. Parents Without Partners (PWP) was a fortuitous choice, and rich with lessons that are still vivid in my memory. I was neither a parent nor divorced at that time, and it might as well have been an experience in a foreign country. The leadership training program I developed for the organization made a difference, but the return for me was heightened awareness and lessons beyond all my experiences.

Trying on new behavior is always a gamble, so go where you have no chips on the table. At least in the beginning. Build your self-confidence and develop trust in your instincts where it's safe to do so. Once you see how easy it is and how successful you are (and how good it feels), you'll be on your way.

A Few Words about Ethics

The literature on management style is often heavy in psychological content. One often-used phrase in particular calls for some reflection: *authentic relationships*. They're the ideal, but keep in mind that there are some people who are not able to be vulnerable, open, and trusting. In group work, I sometimes see a two-tier situation evolving where some in the group are almost aggressive in their openness, while others retreat into non-participation. As always, you must do your best to involve reticent individuals in some way, but be prepared to protect them from the more-aggressive others. Some terrible violations have occurred when well-meaning managers brought authentic relationships and "sharing" into their work groups at levels that some employees were not able to handle. It's critical that every manager consider the limits of each relationship and the constraints that may be necessary to keep the potentially heavy mixture of authority and advanced interpersonal skills under control.

> Make no mistake about this: The elements of a winning management style give power to individuals, as well as emotional leverage; this can put particularly vulnerable direct reports at a disadvantage.

When you want to change your behavioral options to become a more-effective manager, which is perfectly legitimate, stay clear about your motives and your responsibilities.

A manager is in a position of authority; using new-found skills to acquire more power over others usually backfires.

One reason Theory Y has not achieved its potential, in my opinion, is that there have been too many instances in which "feelings" have been over-emphasized in attempts to build more-effective teams. That scares some leaders away from participating in or funding training that has too many "feeling" components.

Now, Go Do It!

Now go out and create your own unique winning management style. Use it to advance your career, make more money for your company, create job security for your team, and help those talented individuals hidden in the organization to rise into roles where they can make more-substantial contributions.

Above all, remember that an improved management style will help you win at work as you help the organization. You will be better able to contribute to management's effort to align the motives and energies of everyone in the organization so that challenging goals can be achieved. Then your organization will have a chance to survive and continue to contribute when many won't.

Go back through this guide and look at what you underlined. Read it again. Look at the places where you made check marks, and remember the questions you had. Now answer them, using the information in this book. The opportunity is out there.

In between here and there is your commitment, and your discipline.

References

Berne, Eric. 1964. *Games People Play*. New York: Grove Press.

Harris, Philip R. 2005. *Managing the Knowledge Culture*. Amherst, Massachusetts: HRD Press, Inc.

Maslow, Abraham. 1965, 1998. *Eupsychian Management*. New York: John Wiley & Sons.

McGregor, Douglas. 1960. *The Human Side of Enterprise*. New York: McGraw-Hill Publishing Company.

Peck, M. Scott. 1978. *The Road Less Traveled: A New Psychology of Love, Traditional Values and Spiritual Growth*. New York: Simon and Schuster.

Peck, M. Scott. 1998. *The Different Drum: Community Making and Peace*. New York: Touchstone.

Peters, Thomas J., and Waterman, Robert H. 1982. *In Search of Excellence*. New York: McGraw-Hill.

Sears, Woodrow H. 1984. *Back in Working Order: How American Enterprises Can Win the Productivity Battle*. Glenview, Illinois: Scott, Foresman and Company.

Sears, Woodrow H., and Audrone Tamulionyte-Lentz. 2001. *Succeeding in Business in Central and Eastern Europe: A Guide to Cultures, Markets, and Practices*. Boston: Butterworth-Heineman.

Stack, Jack, and Burlingame, Bo. 1992. *The Great Game of Business: Unlocking the Power and Profitability of Open-Book Management*. New York: Doubleday.

Stack, Jack, and Burlingame, Bo. 2003. *A Stake in the Outcome: Building a Culture of Ownership for the Long-Term Growth of Your Business*. New York: Doubleday.

About the Author

Woodrow H. Sears earned one of the early doctorates in human resource development, studying under Leonard Nadler at Geor~ coined the
term a~ discipline
known nagement,
Woody a Marine
officer; Extension
Service earned a
master' Leadership
Resourc aviorally-
orientec nager and
later th company.
He has range of
industri cies, and
Canadia ments.

A training,
Woody nt, devel-
oping p d interna-
tional c r of *Back*
in *Work* *Win the*
Prod~ o-author
with ~ *Business*
in C~ *Cultures,*
Mark~ 2001),
Wood national
Execu to go to
Lithua ll there.
Conta~ ysears@
yahoo